The Co
Wedding
Organis

The Complete
Wedding Video
Organiser

BY
DAVID OWEN

foulsham
LONDON • NEW YORK • TORONTO • SYDNEY

foulsham
Yeovil Road, Slough, Berkshire SL1 4JH

Other titles in the Wedding Collection:
The Complete Wedding Organiser and Record
Your Guide to Planning the Wedding Day
The Best Man's Organiser
Wedding Speeches & Toasts
Getting it Right: The Best Best Man
Getting it Right: Your Wedding Planner
Getting it Right: Wedding Speeches
Getting it Right: Wedding Etiquette

Disclaimer:
While every effort has been made to ensure the accuracy of all the information contained within this book, neither the author nor the publisher can be liable for any errors. In particular, since laws change from time to time, it is vital that each individual should check relevant legal details for themselves.

ISBN 0-572-01817-7

Special thanks are due to Terry Murray of Advanced Video Services, Lower Heswall, Wirral, for help, advice and inside information which proved invaluable in producing this book.

Phototypeset in Great Britain by Typesetting Solutions, Slough, Berks.
Printed in Great Britain by St. Edmundsbury Press, Bury St. Edmunds.

Contents

CHAPTER 1

The First Steps

Of all the subjects which present themselves to the keen video programme-maker, weddings offer one of the biggest opportunities, and the biggest challenges. Each wedding video is a consequence of the importance of the day. The event itself is full of romance as an occasion when two people promise to commit themselves to a joint future. It contains drama and tension, because all those concerned are so keen that everything should be perfect; and it can also contain humour, because of the contrast between everyone's expectations and the actual reality of the events as they take place on the day. All of the ingredients for a splendidly visual story are there, except for the villain — unless, of course, it's the eternally changeable British weather.

The challenge stems from the unrepeatability, and uncontrollability, of the day. Everyone hopes their wedding will be a once-in-a-lifetime experience, so you have no chance for rehearsals. If you don't get it right on the day itself, you don't have the consolation that you might do better next weekend. Unless you are equipped and experienced enough to do it properly, it might be better not to raise everyone's expectations by promising to record the event on video.

The other difficulty is that you won't be able to fall back on the usual remedy for a shot which doesn't work, a tape which runs out at the crucial moment, an unexpected noise on the soundtrack, or any of the other hazards which normally attend a shooting session. The wedding ritual is going to happen with or without your efforts — all you can do is shoot what happens and try to do it justice. Instead of being a film

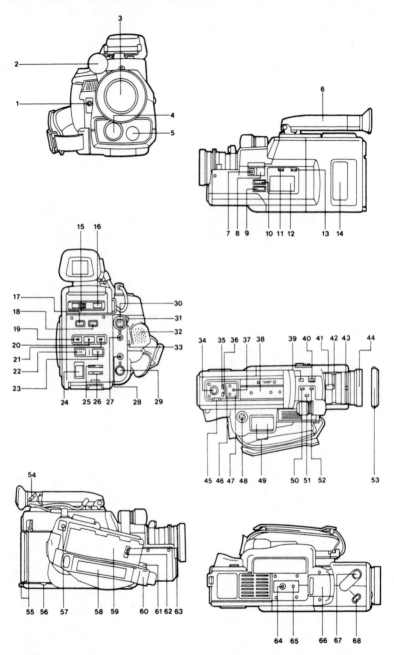

Modern camcorders are a miracle of technology and pack an extensive array of facilities into a typically tiny space. They are also, generally, very easy to use.

1 External microphone jack (MIC)
2 Exclusive microphone
3 Zoom lens
4 Auto-focus sensor window
5 White balance sensor window
6 Electronic viewfinder
7 Full-auto button
8 Focus select button
9 Shutter select button
10 White balance select button
11 Counter memory button
12 Liquid crystal display (LCD)
13 Counter reset button
14 Cassette holder
15 Power switch
16 Recording standby button
17 Monitor button
18 Quick review/edit button
19 Rewind/shuttle search button
20 Play button
21 Fast forward/shuttle search button
22 Pause/still button
23 Stop button
24 Eject switch
25 Standard play/long play recording
    mode select switch
26 Dubbing on/off switch
27 Remote control jack
28 Earphone jack
29 AV connector
30 S-video out connector
31 Alarm on/off switch
32 Thumb rest
33 Recording start/stop button
34 Second recording start/stop button

35 Date/time on/off button
36 Recording time reset button
37 Date/time mode button
38 Viewfinder mount
39 Page button
40 Title on/off button
41 Manual zoom lever
42 Macro button
43 Manual focus ring
44 Lens hood
45 Recording time on/off switch
46 Date/time select button
47 Date/time set button
48 Viewfinder cable connector
49 Power zoom buttons
50 Image reverse button
51 Title memory button
52 Colour button
53 Lens cap
54 Dioptric adjustment control
55 Slots for shoulder strap
56 Tracking control
57 DC In terminal
58 Grip strap
59 Battery mount
60 Lens cap hook
61 Battery pack release lever
62 Video out Switch
63 S-VHS switch
64 Tripod mounting socket
65 Stud hole
66 Clock battery compartment
67 Backlight compensation button
68 Fader button

director, you'll be closer to a news cameraman, trying to capture a sequence of events which you cannot stage or restage. It's your job to shoot a particular part of the day, and be ready to move on in time to set up for the next location and the next stage. If you're not ready, no one is going to wait for you. You'll just have to catch up as quickly as possible, hoping that the gap won't be too noticeable when you come to edit the material. You'll have to plan ahead as carefully as you can, but you will also need to think on your feet like any professional news camera operator who is struggling to keep up with a fast-moving story.

But for all the demands it makes, the rewards of covering a wedding successfully are very real. Apart from the joy a good wedding video gives to the couple involved, and to their families, there's a very real satisfaction in triumphing over the difficulties and setbacks to turn out a polished production. For those people who find they have a flair for this kind of work, there's a very real and expanding market to meet.

It's a task which demands a careful and methodical approach. If you can spot potential snags in advance, it's a great deal easier to find a way of avoiding them. If you do your homework before the great day, you'll save time and enjoy better results when the time comes to start shooting. With most other programme subjects it's not only possible, but also desirable, to learn largely from experience. By making mistakes, and slowly improving the quality of the material you shoot, you will develop your own style and your own methods of working. But each wedding video is unique to the people who form its subject — knowing that a badly produced record of their great day is just part of your learning process isn't going to be much consolation to them.

So the target has to be a professional approach, and a professional programme, from the beginning. This is

Modern camcorders are light, compact and sophisticated. But you need to work to a logical and well-thought-out plan to put the equipment to its best use.

the purpose of the book — to show the complete beginner (or the camcorder enthusiast who may never have made a wedding video before or who, having tried to shoot a wedding, found it surprisingly difficult to do, and the results disappointing) how you can capture the event on cassette and be happy with your finished programme. Because we shall start from the first principles, bear with us if you've already made a long list of programmes and feel happy with your shooting and editing. If that is the case just skip the first three chapters, and rejoin us when we start looking at weddings in particular rather than shooting in general. But everyone who is still trying to come to terms with the technicalities of shooting, of framing, of building up sequences of shots, of editing in-camera or in post-production and of putting together a completed and professional programme on any subject, please stay with us. Professionalism is an approach, and an attitude, which needs to be learned from the moment you first switch the equipment on.

11

First steps to shooting

The first problem we meet is that there is now a very wide range of camcorders and technical formats available on the market. Although the principles are the same, in that all camcorders record their picture and sound information on magnetic tape contained in a cassette — in just the same way as an audio tape recorder converts sounds into electromagnetic signals which are recorded on tape to be replayed when necessary — the width of the tape and the size and configuration of the cassette vary from format to format. Some formats offer more compact cassettes and longer running times from a single cassette — an especially important consideration in shooting weddings, when the chances are you'll need to switch tapes at the most vital moment in the action.

But for the purpose of this book we'll assume you already have the equipment, so that from your point of view the choice has already been made. More important now are the skills and techniques of using it properly to ensure that the sophisticated technology actually helps you produce the pictures you want. So let's begin with the fundamentals of shooting and recording a series of shots of simple, everyday subjects as a guide to using the camera creatively.

The first part of the camcorder to concentrate on is the front end — the optical part of the system, consisting of the lens and the different controls for varying the focus, the aperture and the focal length of the lens combination. Present-day camcorders tend to offer more and more automation; automatic iris, focus, white balance, and so on. In many cases having an automatic facility can actually help, in that it speeds up your ability to respond to changing conditions and it can even make up for any forgetfulness on your part. But the first step to shooting creatively has to be turning off the autofocus facility. Though an automatic focus may seem a good idea in theory, in practice it can get in the way. The principle on which it works is that the camera will focus automatically on whatever object takes up the centre point of the picture. In some cases that may well suit your purpose; in others it won't do at all. For example, let's suppose the main subject of your picture doesn't really occupy the centre of the frame. Taking the wedding theme as an illustration, imagine you're shooting a close-up, head-and-shoulders, portrait-type shot of the bride and groom, so that each occupies one half of the frame. If the area at the centre of the frame (which triggers the autofocus facility) is taken up by the background, the camera will adjust the lens to keep that in focus, so that your two subjects in the foreground will be out of focus — exactly the reverse of what you want.

More serious is the effect of the autofocus on transitional shots. We'll cover these in more detail later, but at this stage all we need realise is how the automatic focus would make them impossible to carry out. A favourite linking shot is the panning shot, where the camera moves sideways from its framing position at the start of the shot to reach another subject which forms the end frame. For example, you might want to pan — again taking a wedding example — from a shot of the nameboard outside the church, to the first of the wedding cars drawing up in the road outside. If you tried to carry out this movement with the automatic focus selected, you may well have the church nameboard in focus at the start of the shot (since this would cover the centre of your frame) but once you start swinging round to pan towards the road, the nameboard will effectively move towards one side of your frame. As soon as it leaves the centre of the frame, the camera will shift focus to sharpen up whatever *is* in centre frame. In all probability this will be the distant background — perhaps the church itself. As soon as the camera reacts to this, the nameboard (which still occupies part of your frame) will swim out of focus and, when the wedding cars appear in the opposite side of your frame as the pan continues, they too will remain out of focus until you've moved far enough for them to be in the centre. Then the autofocusing system will again readjust itself, and the whole character of the scene will change once more.

Change-focus shots — another way of linking two different subjects within the same shot — also become impossible if you're relying on the autofocus. Here the idea is to arrange the two subjects at different distances from the camera, in almost a straight line from the operator's position, so that one is almost behind the other. By carefully adjusting the focus so that one of the subjects is in sharp focus and the other is a vague blur to start the shot, and then by changing the focus setting until the second subject comes into sharp focus as the first one softens into a blur, it's possible to make a smooth and very effective transition. But it does depend on having that manual focus control, which all professional camera operators take for granted as an essential precondition for successful shooting.

How to hold a camcorder

Today's camcorders are miracles of miniaturisation. Where only a decade ago video shooting involved a camera and a separate recorder, linked by a heavy cable and each weighing several times as much as a single camcorder, the average camcorder combination is about the size and weight of one of the old Super 8 cine cameras. This makes it much easier to move quickly when shooting. It also cuts down the very real fatigue problem which still plagues professional crews who have to cope with a lot of heavy items of kit on a location shoot. But, in one respect only, the lightness of the camcorder can create a problem — because it weighs so little, it means the camera operator has to take even greater care to hold it absolutely steady when shooting.

Why is this so important? Play back a typical amateur home video, and one point will strike you immediately. The quality of the pictures, in terms of colour and sharpness, may be surprisingly good. The technical sophistication of today's domestic video equipment is such that high-quality results can be achieved even under the most unpromising conditions. The real difference between an amateur video and professional material is in the way the camcorder is being used — how it's aimed at its subjects, and how it moves from one subject to another.

Most amateur videos (amateur in the sense of the approach, rather than in whether or not the producer is paid for them) suffer from 'hosepipe' shooting. The camera swings backwards and forwards over the scene being shot, then closes in on a particular subject, moves backwards and forwards until the operator finds a focus and framing position to suit, then the picture will wander off in search of another subject altogether. The second subject comes into view, the camera overshoots it, swings back again, homes in on the new subject for a while then, for no apparent reason, swings back towards the original subject again. The result is a sequence which is aimless, boring and difficult to watch because it doesn't have any apparent purpose.

What's needed instead is a properly planned sequence of shots. If, rather than wandering backwards and forwards between the first subject and the second subject, the camera had shown an establishing shot with both subjects in context against the background, those watching it would have understood the way the scene and the subjects fitted together. If the picture had then cut to one of the subjects to make a particular point, then, in turn, to the other subject, the sequence would tell a much more coherent story, and have a much more professional polish. Again, to take our wedding theme as an example, a shot of the bride and groom standing in front of a group of guests, followed by a shot of the bride smiling at her friends, cutting to a shot of the groom waving to some new arrivals, would be much easier and more satisfying to watch than having the camera waving backwards and forwards, covering all those things in one long, unplanned and unstructured recording.

Framing your shots

It's clear that any video sequence has to be built up from a series of individual shots. Now let's stop and look at the way in which those shots are planned and framed, using the camcorder. Begin by checking the machine is switched on, that a cassette has been loaded, that the batteries are fully charged, and that the white balance has been activated. The purpose of this control is to adjust the camcorder to the colour temperature of the available light. We shall cover this in more detail when we look at the factors which affect indoor shooting, but at this stage all we need to remember is that the camera's colour balance needs setting to cope with daylight. In effect, this means adjusting the camera's response to the three colours which, in different combinations, make up all the different hues and tones in the picture — so that white (a combination of equal amounts of all three colours) really does look pure white, without any hint of colour.

Now look through the viewfinder, pick out any subject for a shot and move the focus adjustment to bring the image into sharp relief. Let's assume that we're doing a reconnaissance outside the local church. Point the camera at the church and alter the focus to produce a sharp picture. Now look for the zoom control, which will be a rocker switch, usually mounted on the right side. If you press the front half of the switch (the part nearest the subject you're shooting) then the different lenses which make up the combination lens move relative to one another. Seen through the viewfinder, the effect is that you

Zooming in, from the church and the wrought-iron gate as a long shot (top), to a medium shot of the gate (centre) and a close-up of the wrought-iron detail (bottom).

seem to move closer to the subject. If you were seeing the church gate before, then, at the end of the zoom movement, you might find you're looking at the detail of the wrought iron above it. You'll almost certainly find the picture has shifted out of focus in the meantime. So readjust the focus to bring the image back into sharp relief.

Now press the rearward half of the zoom rocker and watch what happens through the viewfinder. This time you seem to be moving away from the subject so, as the movement continues, the subject becomes smaller and you see more of it in the frame. Where the frame was filled by the detail of the gates, you can see first the gate and then almost the whole church, including part of its tower. You'll also notice that this time the picture stays in sharp focus without the need for any readjustment. Now try that same simple sequence again — but this time record what you're seeing onto the tape.

When you play this sequence back through your television set, so you can see the picture in colour and in detail, you will probably notice two things in particular. A shot which is properly focused at the far end of the zoom — in close-up — stays in focus as you move back to the opposite end of the zoom. The converse doesn't usually happen, and if it does it's a matter of pure coincidence. So, if you actually want to record a shot where you start off showing the whole scene, and intend zooming in to pick out part of that scene in close-up, then you need to zoom in first, set the focus, and zoom out again *before* you start recording. The other point you should be aware of at this stage is that when you're holding the camera in your hands, rather than supporting it on a tripod, any involuntary movements you make will be much more obvious at the close-up end of the zoom. In fact, camera movements which may be perfectly acceptable at the wide end of the zoom — fully zoomed out, as opposed to fully zoomed in at the close-up end of the lens — become awkward and distracting when you zoom in tight.

This means you need to be especially careful about how you hold, and move, the camera. If you hold it too tightly, you'll find it difficult to operate the controls and make the adjustments you need to focus on and frame your subject properly. Not only that, but any slight movement of your body, either because you're not perfectly balanced against a gust of wind, or because whatever you're standing on, or leaning on, moves without warning, will be transmitted straight through to the camera and the picture you're recording. Try instead to insulate the camera from yourself, and everything else, by supporting it rather than gripping it tightly. When you want to move to follow a moving subject, do so slowly, and start and finish the movement by accelerating and decelerating as gently and progressively as you can. Where you can find a secure support to lean on, like a wall or the branch of a tree, use it to help you steady the camera — but make sure it *is* secure before recording anything, or before trusting your weight and your camera to it completely.

Composing your shots

Now let's try looking at some specific subjects, and see how they should be selected and framed within the picture. We'll start with some of the background scenery to our wedding video, and what more appropriate background could there be than a picturesque village church? Later on we'll look at some different ways of getting our shots to include the unusual or the unexpected, but for the time being we'll concentrate on the straightforward establishing shot of the location for the wedding ceremony itself.

First of all pick a suitable camera position. Let's begin by standing just inside the gateway through which arriving guests will walk from the road. Stand to one side, where you'll be clear of people coming and going through the gate, and point your camcorder at the church. Check that the lens is in the fully zoomed-out configuration, check the white-balance facility is appropriately selected, check the tape is loaded and adjust the manual focus to produce a sharp image of the building. Now, what do you see?

Depending on where the gate is situated relative to the church, and depending on the shape of the actual building itself, you may find you have problems in capturing the whole of the church within the frame.

Wherever possible, suit the subject to the shape of the television picture. A side view of the church may not fit as well as an end-on shot.

Remember that, unlike a stills photographer who can have pictures enlarged and then cropped (to isolate the areas of interest) into almost any shape which does them justice, your pictures will always be the same shape — the shape of the television screen itself, the ratio of which is four units wide to three units deep. Because there is no way you can change this restriction (even when you use the zoom facility to reduce or increase the portion of picture you see in the frame the proportions are always the same), all you can do to improve the composition is move your camera position.

Try to compose your picture so that the main features lie on a series of imaginary lines dividing the picture into thirds, vertically and horizontally — or on the intersections between them.

If, for example, the sideways-on view of the church doesn't make a good picture — either because you're only getting part of the building into the frame, or because you have to move so far away that you're missing the detail — try moving round towards one end. Now you're able to capture the whole length of the building in the frame, because it appears fore-shortened from your new camera position. And another advantage may be that you have a strong

21

vertical mass at one side of the picture, in the tower, the spire, or one of the trees in the churchyard, to balance the horizontal lines of the building itself.

Composing a picture is very much a matter of instinct — if it looks right, then usually it *is* right. But there are one or two hints which can help you towards a well-balanced composition, especially when we're looking at landscape and background shots like this. Imagine that the screen, and the viewfinder of your camera, is divided up into thirds; two horizontal lines split the picture into three horizontal layers, and two vertical lines split it into three vertical columns. In other words, your picture is split into nine smaller areas, each one with the same four units wide, three units deep proportions as the full picture.

Now all you have to do is try to frame your picture so that the main features of whatever it is you're looking at lie along the lines, or cut through the intersections between the horizontal dividing lines and the vertical dividing lines. Taking the church as our example, if you arrange the roof of the main building so that it runs along the upper imaginary horizontal line, with the vertical edge of the tower running along the left-hand vertical line, as shown in the sketch on p.21, it will help to ensure a well-balanced composition.

Composing 'people' shots

The same holds good for distant groups of people, where you look at them as a mass of colour rather than as one or two individual faces. But where individuals *are* concerned, it's often better to relate them to the area of the frame as a whole — rather than trying to relate features of the face, or faces (like eyes and mouths) to different dividing lines. For one thing, faces don't have such strong horizontals or verticals as buildings and landscapes do and, for another, they're usually moving sufficiently to throw out any carefully planned composition within seconds.

So what are the rules for people, and people's faces? Instead of striving for an ideal composition, it's easier to avoid one or two definite 'don'ts'. If you're aiming the camera at someone far enough away for you to capture them from head to toe, then make sure you don't appear to chop their feet off at the bottom of the frame, or have the top of their head resting against the top of the frame. In either case the frame will look cramped, and any slight movement of the camera or the subject will have them edging in and out of the frame in a manner which will be distracting to your audience.

If this looks like presenting a problem, then move — further away from your subject, by zooming out more or physically shifting your camera position to give them more room in the frame, or towards them by zooming further in, or taking a step or two nearer. In this case, you won't be going for a full-length shot, but a head-and-shoulders portrait, which will fill the frame better in any case. Distant shots featuring just one person tend to emphasise their isolation, which is fine if that's what you want to suggest, but it won't usually suit the atmosphere of a wedding video. A distant shot of a group of guests or the bridal party — the bride, her father and the bridesmaids — makes for a more animated subject to fill your frame.

If you want to move in closer to capture an individual or a pair of individuals — like the groom, or the groom and the best man waiting to go into the church — then the face, or faces, become your main subject. If each face is small enough in your frame for you to see it whole, then don't cramp your picture by resting chins on the bottom of the frame, ears on the side of the frame, or tops of heads against the top of the frame, for the same reasons as before. Give your subjects room to breathe. Even in cases where you want to come in really close to pick up a sudden smile, or a change of expression, make it clear that you're picking out part of the face with room for it to move, rather than the whole face which is bumping against the limits of the picture every time it, or your camera, moves.

So far we've concentrated on a particular subject — whether people or places — and how to position it in the frame for the best kind of composition. But this is only part of the story. Because the television picture is essentially two dimensional, we need to add the third dimension for ourselves. Take the distant shot of the church we looked at earlier. If the picture simply shows the building in the distance, it will look rather flat and lifeless. If, on the other hand, it's possible to find something in the foreground to give the picture much-needed depth — a path, a bush, a tree, a gateway, a seat, a person or a group of people — then this will help the picture come alive.

When we look at shots of people, the problem of the third dimension becomes slightly different. In most cases the faces of your subjects will be in the foreground, seen against a background which is already in the frame. Here the problem is to keep the two separate, without any irritating juxtapositions between subject and background — watch out for trees or lampposts apparently growing out of your subjects' heads, or any strong horizontal lines apparently sprouting from their ears. All you generally need do to solve the problem is move slightly, or zoom in or out to produce a different relationship between the subject and the background. But you need to be aware of it and able to spot it when it occurs, *before* recording the shot, so you can take the necessary remedial action with the minimum of delay.

Allocating space

There are two more points to consider in picture composition, before we move on to a new chapter and begin defining types of shot. They both relate, in different ways, to this idea of giving a subject enough

Framing the face: leave room above the top of the head and below the chin (top picture). If you move in closer, it's better to leave a gap between the chin and the bottom of the frame (centre) because if the chin rests on the edge of the frame (bottom), it will look cramped and badly composed.

room in the frame. When, for example, we shoot a person looking straight at the camera, there's no hard-and-fast reason why they can't be in the centre of the frame, or slightly to one side or the other. Provided they fit the height limits — and one useful way of ensuring that is to make the bridge of the nose rest on that upper horizontal dividing line we spoke about earlier — the face isn't going to be in danger of reaching the sides of the frame anyway.

But when a face is looking out of the frame, to the left or right, then we need to be careful about where we place our subject. Someone looking to the right of the frame (as seen by you) needs to be placed to the left-hand side of the frame (again, as seen by you). If the picture is composed with the person in the right-hand half of the frame, and they're looking to the right, then they will seem to be peering at the right-hand edge of the picture and the shot won't look

25

'Looking room' (top) and 'walking room' (bottom). Always give your subject room in the frame, in the direction in which they are looking or moving, to prevent cramping the picture.

believable. This is referred to as giving your subject 'looking room'. If your subject is actually moving, then you need to give them room on the side of the frame into which they're moving — this is called giving them 'walking room'.

On the other hand, you need to be careful about giving any of your subjects too much room. Generally speaking, a shot needs to concentrate on the main focus of interest. If that focus of interest is someone reading a book, you would frame it to show the head and shoulders of the person reading, down to their hands holding the book so it's clear what they're doing. You wouldn't pull so far back that the person and the book occupied the centre of the frame, with a large dead area surrounding them. Alternatively, if the focus of interest was to be the book itself, then you would come in closer and concentrate on the hands of the reader and the pages of the book. It might even be that the real focus of interest was a particular line of text, or even a particular word, and you would need to come in closer still. It all depends on the context of the shot and the message you are trying to convey to your audience.

It's important to remember that composition is an area where practice can go a long way towards making things perfect. If you begin by being aware of the rules we've covered in this chapter, you'll find they can provide useful guidance in the direction of securing well-framed and well-composed shots, and useful warnings of the chief dangers and problems. But don't forget that the rules are not sacred and can always be broken when you have good reason. As you become more practised at shooting different subjects, you'll find that you become more adept at composing each picture instinctively. When *that* happens — when you find you can react to a new subject quickly and smoothly, without having to stop to think about the do's and don'ts of putting the picture together — then you can begin to consider the different types of shots, how and when to use them and how to link them together to make a sequence which will keep the audience interested and do your production justice. We'll cover these topics in the next chapter.

Shooting with a Purpose

So far we have looked at the factors which need to be taken into account when framing and composing shots of particular subjects. Now we're going to look at the broad classifications which are applied to describe the different types of shot which are used in a production, and the reasons for using each one in a given situation. And we'll begin with the shot of a church that we looked at earlier, from a composition point of view.

Let's assume that you have set up your camcorder in a similar position to the one we used to show the effect of the zoom lens. This time, zoom out as far as the lens on your camcorder will allow. Different models have different zoom ratios (commonly 6 to 1, or 8 to 1) between the focal length of the lens combination in the fully zoomed-in position, and the focal length of the lens combination in the fully zoomed-out position. What these ratios mean to the camcorder operator is, broadly speaking, the extent of the apparent movement forwards or backwards between the two extremes. The greater the ratio, the longer the zoom range will be.

In this case we'll assume that the fully zoomed-out position provides you with the whole church in the frame. In shot-listing terms, this would be described as a long shot of the church, and would usually be abbreviated in a script or shot list to 'LS church'. Confusingly, the same shot could also be described as a wide shot (abbreviated to 'WS church'). These terms are well-nigh interchangeable and the description you'd actually use depends on personal preference and, perhaps, the quality which best sums up the shot. If the composition was arranged so that the

Three different framings of the same shot, secured using the zoom lens. At the top is a long shot of the church, in the centre a medium shot of the church and tower and at the bottom a close-up of the tower clock.

third dimension we looked at in the previous chapter was particularly obvious, it would be more likely to be described as a long shot. If, on the other hand, the principal subject of your shot was seen in the middle of a broad sweep of landscape or scenery, then it might be better described as a wide shot.

Now zoom in to the fully zoomed-in position showing the clock halfway up the church tower. By contrast with the long (or wide) shot, this is a close-up shot, and would be abbreviated to 'CU clock'. But everything is relative. This particular shot would be described as a close-up in relation to the previous shot because it appears at the opposite end of the zoom. But if we had positioned the camera much closer to the church, so that the framing of the picture was identical, but this time we were seeing it at the fully zoomed-out position of the lens combination, then it could be described, just as accurately, as a long shot of the church clock. If we then zoomed in from that position, the close-up end of the zoom might easily show us one of the numerals, and *that* would be described as 'CU numeral'. The context of a shot is as important as its content in determining exactly what type of shot it is.

Now let's assume we have stayed in our original camera position, which gives us the option of a long shot of the church at the fully zoomed-out position, and a close-up of the church clock at the fully zoomed-in position. If we now move to approximately the mid-point of the zoom, we'll see a shot with more or less intermediate framing between the two extremes we've just described. This might, for instance, show the church tower, half the main building of the church, and a little bit of the foreground. It would be described, in relation to the other two shots, as a medium shot and would be abbreviated to 'MS church'.

These are the three basic descriptions which can be used to classify shots in relation to one another. But there are occasions when you want slightly more detailed ways of describing a shot which may involve you moving further back than for one which has already been classified as a medium shot. In our example, this might mean moving further back to enable the whole of the church to appear in the frame, but without showing as much of the surroundings as in the long-shot framing. Since this represents a step backwards from the medium shot to the long shot, it's usually described as a medium long shot and, in this case, it would be abbreviated to 'MLS church'.

Similarly, there are different types of close-up which may need to be differentiated from one another. If we define our view of the church clock filling the frame as our close-up shot, then a slightly more distant view — stopping short of our full close-up, with the clock smaller in the frame and more of the tower showing — would be described as a medium close-up, and abbreviated to 'MCU clock' or 'MCU tower'.

If we then moved so that we were able to concentrate on, say, the hands of the clock and the numerals from 1 to 5 in the frame, this could be described as a big close-up shot, which would be abbreviated to 'BCU clock', or, more accurately, 'BCU numerals'. If we then moved in closer still to pick out, say, the end of the minute hand and one of the numerals, this would be an extreme close-up, abbreviated to 'ECU figure'. As we emphasised earlier, these descriptions are all relative, and each depends very much on the context of a shot in terms of its position in a sequence covering that particular subject.

Two-shots and three-shots

All these shot descriptions can be used for any kind of subject, whether it's a building, a landscape, a vehicle or a person. But when we're covering a whole series of shots of people at an event such as a wedding, or in an interview, there's another kind of classification which, when applied, can actually be a positive help in keeping shot sequences varied and interesting. It's also very simple.

Let's begin with a shot of a single person. In our wedding example it might be the bridegroom standing outside the church waiting to enter. If no one else is standing near him, we are free to frame him as a close-up (head only), a medium close-up (head and shoulders), a medium shot (top half down to the waist or thereabouts) or even a long shot. Let's now assume he's joined by the best man. Frame them both in the same shot and we have a two-shot. Because the geometry of the frame is fixed, fitting both faces into that frame is going to impose its own limitations on the shot, so the description is quite a precise one. If they're then joined by one of the guests, we can frame them as a three-shot (provided they're standing close together) and, if more guests join the group, then we're looking at a group shot. Again, because of the limitations of the frame, fitting all of the group into the shot is going to force you to pull back from your original close-up framing to something like a medium shot. But the group shot is a useful classification, as it describes exactly what you expect to see in the frame.

But how does that help us to plan our shooting in sequence terms? When you think of parts of the wedding day when the bridal party and the guests are all together in the same location — either at the reception, or on leaving the church when the formal photographs are being taken and the remainder of the guests are looking on — you will need to concentrate very much on people in their different groups and arrangements. Part of the purpose of a good wedding video, as we'll see later on, is to show not only the principal people involved, but also views of their friends and relatives having a good time. This means providing a round-up of people doing broadly similar things: talking to one another, eating and drinking, watching the photographs being taken, or listening to the speeches being delivered. As this will involve a whole sequence of shots on the same theme, how do you go about keeping them varied and interesting? The answer is that you vary the framing as far as possible. Pick an individual close-up to start off the sequence perhaps, then go for a three-shot, then a two-shot, then a group shot, and so on. Even though all your shots are of people's faces, the distances from the camera and the number of people in each shot will all be different. If you also find (as you almost certainly will) that they're looking in different directions as well, then you have all the essentials for a good sequence of varied shots, simply by counting the number of people featured in each one, and making sure that the number changes from shot to shot.

Linking shots — the pan

We'll go into more detail about building up sequences later, and we'll also cover the kind of objectives you need to keep in mind for different stages of the wedding itself, and the day's events. For the time being we'll limit ourselves to looking at single shots, and their place in recording whatever is happening at each part of the proceedings. Up to now, as far as this chapter in particular is concerned, we have been looking at the different types, classifications and descriptions of shots with static frames. We'll now move on to another type of shot — the type which, because of the camera movement involved, can be used to link two different subjects, or two different parts of the same subject, within a single shot.

The first of this type of shot is one we described earlier, as an example of the need for focusing to be under the camera operator's control: the panning shot. This involves a move from an opening frame to an entirely different framing position by turning the camera horizontally on its tripod, or by carrying out a similar movement with a hand-held camera. The

A bird's-eye view of your trial pan, from the church noticeboard to the doorway.

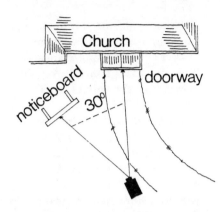

example we used before involved panning from the noticeboard in front of the church to the road outside, as we might do when the bridal party is due to arrive. Now let's look at that type of shot from a slightly different point of view.

We're going to start, as before, with a pan from the church noticeboard — but this time we're going to end on a framing which doesn't depend on people being in shot, as we want to be able to practise the shot at any time. Instead, we shall try panning from the noticeboard to the doorway of the church, which requires a slightly different camera position. Move to a point where you can see the noticeboard and the doorway at roughly similar distances, but far enough apart for the camera not to be able to frame both at the same time. You don't want them too close or the pan will be too short, and if they're too far apart it will seem to go on for ever. Perhaps an ideal would be a pan of around 30 degrees. Try to imagine you're looking down at the scene from above — a bird's-eye view — and the camera is at the centre of an imaginary clock-face, with the noticeboard at the twelve o' clock position. The ideal is for the doorway of the church to be at the one o' clock position. You may need to shift your camera position relative to the doorway and the noticeboard in order to achieve this arrangement.

Now aim the camera at the noticeboard, choose your framing, and adjust the focus to produce a sharp picture. Swing round through your thirty-degree arc and see how the church doorway appears in the viewfinder. It should be in focus, as one of your objectives was to arrange your positioning so both noticeboard and doorway were at similar distances from your camera, but you also need to check the framing to make sure the shot you end up with has been properly composed.

If it isn't — if, for example, you need to open out the framing by zooming back a little — then make the adjustment and pan back to find the noticeboard, checking the effect of your new framing on the opening part of your shot. You may feel this too is less than ideal, so try to find a compromise whereby the same zoom setting will do for both ends of the pan (what camera operators refer to as the opening and closing frames of the pan). With greater experience you can combine a pan with a zoom, so you can vary your framing to suit both ends of the shot to perfection, but for the time being it's better to accept the need for compromise, and master one movement at a time.

Now aim the camera at the opening frame of your pan — the noticeboard — and start recording. Wait for a second or two, then move slowly sideways until the church doorway comes into your frame. When you reach the closing frame, stop moving the camera, wait a second or two, then hit the 'pause' button. Try the pan several more times, striving always to make the movement as slow and as smooth as possible, with no jerkiness or camera shake. Then play the results back over your television screen, so you can see them as you would view them as part of a finished programme.

You may find your pans look good right from the beginning. What's more likely, as a beginner, is that

The trial pan
as seen
through the
viewfinder;
from the
noticeboard
(top), past the
gate (centre)
to the doorway
(bottom
picture).

the camera movement starts with a perceptible jump and the pan itself is too fast. All too often we begin by moving the camera as we would move our eyes, and the result is a confused blur between the opening frame and the closing frame. What's really needed is a very slow movement indeed, with a smooth and gradual transition from the stationary starting point into the pan, a smooth, slow and steady movement during the course of the pan, then a smooth slowing down so that the camera finally stops with the closing shot safely in the frame. Another problem is the tendency to concentrate so hard on the slowness and steadiness of the pan that you overshoot your closing frame and either have to stop suddenly, or even move back slightly — both very definitely to be avoided. One way of guarding against this is to keep your other eye open (the one not looking into the viewfinder) so that you are aware of a wider context than that afforded by the restricted field of view of the viewfinder frame.

Describing all this is simple — achieving it is more a matter of painstaking practice. Try it over and over again until you're able to attain the smooth movement you want, with a camcorder which is hand-held, mounted on a tripod, or both. Once the technique is mastered properly, you should be able to pan at will whenever you see two subjects which would benefit from a shot which succeeds in linking them.

The tilt shot

Not all pans are horizontal pans ('pan left' or 'pan right' in a camera script). It's also possible to pan from one subject to another vertically in a 'pan up' or 'pan down'. For example, let's imagine we wished to tie a specific stage in the wedding — like the posing for the formal group photographs at the foot of the church tower — to a particular time of the day. An easy way of doing this would be to use the church clock as the opening frame, and then pan slowly down the tower to the group being marshalled by the wedding photographer at its foot. Alternatively, you may want to show the passing of time between the taking of the photographs and the arrival at the reception, without being able to include a sequence of shots of the actual departure and arrival. An effective way of doing this would be to pan upwards from the photographs being taken, to reveal the church clock as your closing frame. By making your next picture in the finished sequence a clock at the reception, you make the point about the change of time and place simply, economically and clearly.

Vertical pans — also, confusingly, sometimes called tilt shots as in 'tilt up' or 'tilt down' — need as much care as horizontal pans to make them smooth, even and polished. With practice, and growing confidence, it's even possible to carry out pans which are combinations of vertical and horizontal. An example of this would be the pan needed to link the church clock in the tower with the taking of the photographs outside the main door of the church, where the frame has to be moved downwards and sideways to end in the right place. In cases like these, the both-eyes-open procedure is essential to making sure you hit the right target at the end of the pan, without needing any sharp changes of direction to correct your aim during the course of the pan itself.

If you're trying to carry out pans like these with a hand-held camera — especially one of today's light and compact camcorders — the secret is to try to move yourself and the camera as a single unit. Don't simply tilt the camera up and down, or move it to one side or the other, while keeping your body still. It's better to move with the camera, leaning backwards from the waist as you tilt it upwards, bending forwards as you tilt it down, swinging slowly round as you pan right to left. By moving yourself and the camera in combination it will be easier to achieve those smooth, slow, balanced movements than it will if you move the camera alone.

The zoom shot

The other principal type of linking shot is more familiar, because we've been using the zoom facility as an aid to framing single shots properly. But zoom shots also comprise another powerfully useful technique for linking two subjects in a single take — and, since we're now dealing in almost every case with a power-driven movement, a zoom is very often easier for a beginner striving to achieve a smooth transition between the chosen subjects.

At their simplest, however, zoom shots impose a different type of discipline from pans and tilts, in terms of the subjects you choose and how you actually link them. For example, a natural use for a zoom shot is to relate a particular close-up to its surroundings. Imagine you have the bridesmaids standing outside the church waiting for their turn to be photographed after the ceremony is over. Your opening frame, at the close-up end of the zoom, might be a bouquet held by one of the bridesmaids. By zooming out, and keeping the camera steady, you can either end the zoom on a mid shot of the bridesmaids as a group, or you can continue zooming right out to a long shot of the church, with the wedding party spread out in the foreground while the pictures are taken. The choice is up to you, and will depend on the point you wish to make and the next shot in your planned sequence. We will look at sequencing in the next chapter, but for the moment the main criterion is to be sure you know where you want your zoom to end, and to make sure you end it there smoothly and decisively. Don't have second thoughts and restart the zoom after you'd stopped it — that fatal air of indecision is a failing of so many amateur videos. If you want to react to changing circumstances which might mean lengthening or shortening a zoom, be sure you take the decision with time to spare.

Now let's consider, in a little bit more detail, the requirements of a successful zoom as a linking device

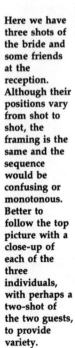

Here we have three shots of the bride and some friends at the reception. Although their positions vary from shot to shot, the framing is the same and the sequence would be confusing or monotonous. Better to follow the top picture with a close-up of each of the three individuals, with perhaps a two-shot of the two guests, to provide variety.

between subjects. The pull-out from a bouquet to a group of people is an example of a 'zoom-out' shot — but the 'zoom in' can be just as effective in a different way. Imagine that you begin with a wide-shot framing of a large group of wedding guests on a sunny day outside the hotel where the reception is being held. You want to concentrate on the bride and groom as they move around greeting all their friends for the first time since the ceremony itself finished. A zoom would be an ideal way of carrying out this link as, in a single shot, you can pick out your principal subjects and concentrate more and more closely on them. A straight cut from the long shot, full of people, to a close-up of the two in the middle of the throng would, in many ways, be far less effective.

How is a shot like this recorded? Pick your subject in close-up, and check the focus before zooming out to find the opening frame. Then start recording; wait for a second or so and begin the zoom in, correcting the aim where necessary to frame your chosen subjects just as you want them. In other words, the order in which you do things is zoom in, check framing and focus, zoom out to check the opening frame, start recording, zoom in, end on your chosen framing and then pause at the end of the shot — allowing a second or so for the close-up image to establish itself properly first.

These are two points worth remembering in a zoom-in shot like this — you need to pick a subject which is unlikely to move far enough to be out of your chosen framing before you finish the zoom, and you need to keep your other eye open to check the surroundings to your shot. This way you'll notice if things are starting to move, giving you the opportunity to move with them by including a slight pan in your zoom, to pick up a different end frame but still achieve the results you want. This combined movement is a great deal easier to manage with a hand-held camera than it would be with anything but a camera mounted on a very high-quality and well-adjusted tripod — though in this case it would involve a less natural and instinctive movement. The keynote, as always, is to keep all the movements as smooth and gradual as possible. In this way, your reaction to unexpected movements will strike your audience as the result of confident, professional pre-planning, which is exactly the feeling you want your finished programme to convey.

Where else can zoom shots be used? Generally speaking, in any situation where you want to zoom in to a particular part of your opening shot, or where you want to zoom out of a particular subject to show it in its wider context. But you can also use zooms to reveal an unexpected relationship between your opening subject and its wider context — for example, you might zoom out of a shot of the bride preparing to throw her bouquet, to a waiting group of friends who are not shown in the original framing. As you pull out, the wider frame shows you're shooting over the heads of those waiting to catch the bouquet and, with a little luck and some careful timing, you may well capture the throwing and the catch in wide shot at the end of your zoom.

The change-focus shot

If you add a pan up, down or sideways to the basic zoom shot, you can also cope with linking subjects which are not so ideally in line — relative to your camera position — as those used in the pure zoom would need to be. But if the subjects *are* in line, with one of them much closer to the camera than the other, you have another useful linking shot at your disposal — and that's the change-focus shot.

This works best when the nearer subject still enables you to see the subject which is further away from you, either through or around it. Examples of an ideal first subject might be a wrought-iron gate, a flowering shrub, or the leaves on the branch of a tree — through each of which you can see the second subject, such as the guests on the lawn outside the reception hall. To make the change-focus shot work well, you need to pick your camera position with care. You need to be close enough to the nearer subject for it to be completely out of focus when you have the background scene sharply in focus. In other words, you want the distance between the two subjects to be greater than the depth of field of your lens (the range within which all objects seen will be in sharp focus at the same time), in the light conditions in which you're working. Since the depth of field varies with ambient light, this will be greater out of doors on a sunny day than it will be either in dull weather or indoors — so

A change-focus shot: from the church in soft focus and the gateway in sharp focus (top) to the gateway out of focus and the church in sharp relief (bottom).

in bright conditions you will have to move closer to your first subject for the shot to work than you would have to in darker surroundings.

You also need to pay attention to how the two subjects appear in the frame when you compose the shot. Ideally the nearer subject should take up approximately half the frame (if you are seeing over it or around it, rather than through it, as would be the case with the wrought-iron gate example), leaving you free to see the second subject in the other half of the frame.

When recording the shot, your frame would normally remain static. All you need do is record a second or so of your opening frame (once you've decided whether you want to go from your near subject in focus to your farther subject in focus, or vice versa), and then slowly turn the focus ring on your lens, taking great care to keep the camera as steady as possible. (This is one shot which is usually easier to do with the camera securely mounted on a tripod, or resting on some convenient surface, to help you keep it steady while concentrating on the focus adjustment.) Once the second subject is sharply in focus, wait a second or so for the image to establish itself before ending the recording.

This all sounds a trifle complicated and, certainly, change-focus shots do need more careful planning and setting up than simple zooms and pans. For this reason you really need to pick subjects which aren't going to move while you're setting up, or you may find that the purpose of your clever change-focus shot has disappeared by the time you begin shooting it. On the other hand, you don't want them to be too static. Since the nearer subject needs to be still enough for you to shoot through it, or around it, it's best if the object which is further away from the camera has enough movement in it for the audience to see something is happening, even while the image itself is still out of focus. That way you can add to the dramatic effect, which is the strong point of this kind of shot when it's done well. But, like all other dramatic effects, don't over-use it — you risk wasting time, and boring your audience.

These are the basic shots, the building blocks from which you will construct your finished video of the wedding, and we shall return to them at different times in discussing the action needed to cover each phase of the proceedings. For the time being, though, we're going to leave the action side of production (though constant practice is a must if your selection and execution of shots is going to be skilled and automatic enough to keep up with events as they unfold — without the luxury of a prepared script to which everyone will adhere, and which you can shoot and record at your own pace). Instead, we're going to look at the essential tasks of planning and doing a recce of your subject (as applied to a wedding video), before we look at how those plans can be turned into reality.

But first, we need to consider our treatment. Given that the nature of the wedding — from the ritual used in the service to the traditions of the reception and the speeches, and the expectations of those involved — is largely fixed, the treatment on which the programme is based will depend on what we want it to do. And that means considering what a wedding video ought to be: what its objectives should be, and the style which should be used to realise those objectives. For example, we need to consider what should be included and what should be left out — either on the grounds of coping with events, or in the interests of keeping the finished programme brisk and entertaining. We even need to consider what kind of audience the programme is being aimed at, just as we would with any other kind of video programme. Above all, we need to strike the right kind of balance between covering every detail of the great day (even if that were possible) and making an interesting and entertaining programme.

What is a Wedding Video?

Before starting to plan out the shooting of a wedding video in detail, it's sensible to stop to consider the treatment. This means asking the question: 'What is a wedding video?' Or, more precisely, what should a wedding video set out to do, how should it aim to do it, and what should it not attempt to do in the interests of both its producer and its audience?

Most people involved in a wedding will probably each have a different perspective on the role a wedding video should play, and the subject matter it should include. Some couples feel it should include absolutely everything. Every conceivable detail of the great day should be there, playing its part in a real-time reproduction of the whole order of events, from getting up in the morning to the closing down of the disco at the end of the night, long after the couple themselves have said goodbye to their friends and left on their honeymoon.

Unfortunately, taking this approach results in an exhausting day for the programme-maker, and a less than perfect one for everyone else. Setting out to cover everything with a single camcorder and normal commercial tapes means having to bend the time-table to suit the camera's availability. If two parts of the event are likely to happen simultaneously, then one of them has to be left out — or it has to be restaged, with all the problems of artificiality and the danger of knock-on delays affecting other parts of the timetable.

There's also the question of the audience to consider. Shooting absolutely everything would be a total impossibility — even trying to cover most of the action would generate several hours of material. The result would be a programme which would lose its appeal all too quickly, even for the couple involved. How many people want to sit down in front of a four- or five-hour video programme, even if they are watching their own wedding? Its appeal for friends, relatives and guests alike would also be severely limited. Watching it once would be a duty, watching it again in its entirety would definitely be something to be avoided at all costs.

The point to remember is that real life, even on the day of a wedding, can be full of boring pauses while everyone is waiting for something to happen — the arrival of the cars, the start of the service, the serving of the soup, or the finishing of the speeches. At the time, we're often unaware of these intervals where little or nothing is happening, because we can talk to relatives, sit in the sunshine, enjoy a drink, or wave to friends at the other side of the room. But sitting in the living room watching it all in remorseless detail on the screen provides no such escape, and a minute which would have passed quickly and unremarkably on the day itself, seems to drag interminably when seen as part of a programme.

The basic approach

So, deciding the overall approach is first and foremost your job. Your audience may not be aware of these considerations in advance, though they'll certainly be aware of them when they've watched the programme right through from beginning to end. It's up to you to explain all this, and advise them how long you think the programme should last, balancing its enjoyment value with their own wishes to have a detailed and permanent reminder of the great day.

What's an acceptable compromise? In most cases video programmes need to be brief to be successful. A promotional programme might be best at around five to ten minutes in length, where you need to capture the audience's attention and put over your message without risking them becoming bored. A training programme might be twice as long — 15 to 20 minutes — if you have a reasonable amount of detailed information to convey to your audience, who have a duty to watch the material you're putting on the screen. Entertainment, where the audience has no particular involvement with the subject of the programme, but where its contents are intrinsically interesting, can vary in length from 15 minutes to an hour and a half — sometimes even longer. Where in all this does the average wedding video fit?

In one respect, the audience is involved with the subject of the video because, in most cases, they were present at the event themselves and, in others, because at least they'll know the people who did attend. That suggests the programme could go into more detail, and last longer, than programmes where this would not be a consideration. But, on the other hand, the story of the day itself is entirely familiar — the ritual of the service and the kind of speeches and toasts made at the reception will be known from legions of other weddings. So there's no suspense in the story, and everyone knows how it will turn out — especially if they were there on the day. The interest lies in seeing familiar faces and familiar places in the unfamiliar context of the television screen, particularly if professional standards of shooting, picture composition, editing and dubbing have conspired to produce a high-quality result.

Taking all these factors into account, a sensible comparison would be with a high-quality documentary, or even a feature film, where a length set somewhere between an hour and an hour and a half is within an acceptable range. Provided you start out with these limits in mind, explain your reasoning to your audience, and make your plans accordingly, the chances are that you will end up with a programme which is long enough to cover all of the essentials, and still short enough to provide entertaining and acceptable viewing.

Deciding the overall target length of your programme will influence the way in which you set out to capture the different parts of the event during the course of the day. But before we look into the planning phase in more detail, there's another question to consider. In most video productions the best way to achieve a professional result is for you, the programme producer, to act as the director as well — making sure people move at the right moment for the camera, stop at the right spot, say the right things and stop when you're ready to end the shot, will all help in making for a polished production with a minimum of editing afterwards. Whether the production is an ambitious documentary, or an original story, it's the only way to put the programme together.

But weddings, as we said at the beginning, are different. They have all kinds of ingredients which help to make the day happy, enjoyable and successful, and generally speaking the sight of the camcorder operator getting in the way isn't one of them. The more you interrupt the action to get into the right camera position, to move your lights, or to ask someone to repeat what they've just done 'for the benefit of the camera', the more you're going to become an unwelcome intrusion into the day's events. Every pause in the action, every request for a repeated movement, or a different turn of phrase, is going to help destroy that very spontaneity which would otherwise be one of your strongest allies. Every extra light, or unnecessary pause while you and your camcorder move position, is going to help turn a genuine event — your friends' wedding — into a video production on the theme of a wedding, with your friends cast as extras. No matter how polished the result, the chances are you wouldn't be thanked for it, nor would you deserve to be.

Your best approach is to adopt the old fly-on-the-wall technique so popular among present-day documentary programme-makers. Your job should be to make a selection from the day's sights and sounds to tell the story of the wedding as effectively, and as unobtrusively, as you can. Ideally, your subjects shouldn't even know you're there. They may spot you and your camcorder and, at first, be influenced by the idea that what they say and do is going to be captured and played back over the television screen. But the demands of the day, and all they have to concentrate on to make sure everything runs properly, are going to reduce you to part of the background — along with all the guests using still cameras to take snapshots of the wedding for the family album.

And this is the way it should be. The best definition of a good wedding video is that it should be a moving-pictures-and-sound equivalent of the traditional wedding photo album, to be taken out and browsed through in later years, as a reminder of a happy and important day. When that happens, it won't be any clever camera tricks, or complex staged sequences, that will capture your audience's hearts — their value will fade with repetition. What will matter, and what will make your programme precious as a source for happy reminiscences, are the spontaneous touches and glimpses of people reacting to, and being a part of, the day's events. The more invisible you and your camera can be, the more accurately and convincingly you will capture those elusive qualities — and the better your programme will become.

Coping with the unexpected

Now, let's move on to specifics. Without the luxury of being able to run the action to suit yourself, you and your camcorder will have to work harder, anticipating what's likely to be important, and avoiding anything which is likely to be tedious. This is the reason for the emphasis on practice in the two earlier chapters —

practising framing, and practising effective and economical linking shots until they become semi-automatic and you can respond quickly and effectively to each opportunity you see. In fact, the more you practise, the more likely you are to recognise an opportunity for an unusual and effective shot, and the more likely you are to be able to capture it in the short amount of time you'll inevitably have.

However, even the most experienced camera operator is going to end up with some material which is less than ideal. You may set up for a shot, start recording, and find that you have a false start — because your subject suddenly remembers to stop and have a word with someone in the crowd before walking into your frame. You may find that a particular pan doesn't quite come off, and you quickly have to replace it with another shot. Modern camcorders are very clever at being able to assemble-edit one shot onto the end of another — editing in-camera — but if you're totally dependent on this facility, you're something of a prisoner of what you're able to shoot on the day, and from moment to moment. If you have to go back and overlay a shot which doesn't work properly with a better alternative, it's all going to take time and, when you're ready for the new shot, you may have missed an ideal, and unique opportunity.

The only real solution is to be able to edit after you have finished recording all the material — in post-production, as the professionals say. This doesn't necessarily call for a lot of expensive equipment, although anyone seriously interested in the wedding-video market should consider the value of some extra kit in enhancing flexibility and programme quality. All you really need are the connections which allow you to hook up your camcorder to your home VCR, and edit your programme from the camera tapes onto a master cassette in the recorder. This makes all the difference to the ease, and the success, with which you can cover the event, and we'll go through the

The father of the bride — look for candid shots which show his pride and pleasure at quiet moments during his daughter's special day.

Check out the site for the reception on your recce — and make a note of important details, like trees which may screen your view of the doorway.

procedure in detail later. All you need to remember for the moment is that, with this kind of facility in mind, you don't need to shoot everything in the order in which it will actually appear in the finished programme — a most precious freedom for you; the programme-maker.

Research and priorities

The other need is for research. You need to know as much as you can about where and when the wedding is taking place; everything from the name of the church, the address and the potential for parking problems on the day, to the time the groom, the best man, the guests and the bridal party are expected to arrive. You need to know the best route to the reception, the journey time, and the wedding-day parking arrangements, and you also need to know where and when the official photographs will be taken, and by whom. Very often you can rely on the professional photographer to do two jobs for you. It's part of his task to direct people into the right groups for the formal pictures, and you can shoot them as he collects them together. Secondly, you can also look for candid shots of people reacting to his efforts to marshal them into line — and persuade them to smile for his camera as well as yours — provided you stay out of his way and profit discreetly from all his hard work and organising ability.

The best place to find out all this preliminary information is from the people responsible for setting up the event — the bride and her family. This presents an excellent opportunity to talk about what the video is going to include, so your most important customers know exactly what to expect. The first step is to decide what your priorities are. Most wedding-video customers would probably agree on the highlights — those parts of the day's events which must be included in full. First come the wedding vows made in the church, the chapel or the registry office; secondly, the speeches — or the principal speeches at least — with the toasts to the bride and groom, the bridesmaids and so on. Another possibility is the reading of the greetings cards and messages by the best man, and another, the departure of the bride and groom at the end of the reception — a fitting conclusion to the whole programme.

In addition to these highlights, customers will have different ideas on the extras they'd like included. A sequence at the wedding rehearsal, a sequence of the bride and groom getting ready in their respective homes, the arrival of the groom, best man and the guests at the church, the bride and her father getting into the car for the trip to the church, the entry of the bridal party — all these things (or most of them at least) are possible with a certain amount of careful advanced planning.

As far as the reception is concerned, possibilities include the arrival of the bride and groom, shots of the receiving line greeting the guests as they arrive (assuming this is part of the event) and candid shots of the guests relaxing with drinks before they take their places at the tables. Shots of the meal being served, of the guests eating and responding to the toasts, of the cake being cut, and of the departure of the bride and groom, provide a pretty full list of priorities for the programme producer. If you can cover most of these, the chances are you'll have the material for a comprehensive and varied programme which will do justice to the day.

The beginning and the end

Of course, some weddings don't stop there. It's becoming increasingly popular to organise a dance or a disco in the evening for the guests, at which the bride and groom may put in an appearance before they finally leave on their honeymoon. Some couples might want this to be included in a wedding video, but it's definitely worth trying to point out the difficulties. Disco lighting — a combination of romantic gloom with over-bright special effects — is a nightmare for a video camera to cope with and, in terms of the footage it produces, presents probably the worst conditions it's possible to imagine.

Another limitation is that most of the dancing will be done by a fraction of guests who have the energy to keep going when everyone else has wilted, so it's difficult to capture a great variety of people which will do justice to the occasion. Thirdly, an evening disco doesn't have the unique quality which the actual wedding has — in visual terms. It's just another party, and any material you include will have to justify its place in your finished programme. If you're strict about the running-time, and you have a lot of good material from the rest of the day, then using ten minutes of disco dancing will mean you have to leave out ten minutes of the wedding to make room for it, which might be a pity.

Let's assume that you and your clients can agree on where and how the programme should end. We now need to consider how it should begin. In the interest of brevity some wedding videos open on shots of the church or the invitations, together with the opening titles, and the audience is caught up in the drama of the ceremony from the very beginning. But it's also worth thinking about a more leisurely beginning, effectively telling the audience 'the story so far'. Both bride and groom have been growing up for 20 years or more before reaching this important moment in their lives, and the chances are that their life stories have already been recorded visually in the pages of the family photograph albums.

So ask to have a look at the pictures available. If they like the idea, sort out a selection of stills from babyhood onwards, including pictures taken at school (even formal group photos if the face of the

The evening disco; a nightmare for a camcorder, with its low background lighting contrasting harshly with random bright spots.

individual we're going to concentrate on can be made out in some detail), family holiday snaps, pictures taken at college or on trips abroad, pictures with friends (who may well also be at the wedding), with relatives and with parents. Try to pick a fairly even spread over the years, with approximately the same number for both bride and groom, and note them in chronological order. We'll cover how to blend them into the complete programme later. What you need to know at this stage is whether or not the bride and groom would like this kind of introduction to the video, and whether sufficient picture material is available to make it varied and interesting.

This is also a good time to make a note of some of the facts and figures about the wedding: how many guests are expected, how many of each immediate family, how many friends, how many relatives, and what are the priorities for capturing shots of the guests if the wedding is to be a large one? If you find at this stage that you're likely to have a lot of rushing about to do simply keeping up with your shooting priorities, then it's worth giving some thought to arranging to have an assistant. The assistant need not take over any of the shooting, but simply help you with carrying tapes, batteries and tripod, parking the car, moving lights and microphones, watching for arrivals and departures, and all the other time-consuming chores there will be, over and above recording the actual material.

Thinking in sequences

Finally, before beginning the detailed planning, it's worth giving some thought to how you intend telling the story in terms of picture sequences. This is another case of wedding videos being different from most other video productions, in two respects. You have a subject (and a story) which is totally familiar to all who will watch it — apart from the very youngest, and there will be plenty of people to explain to them the significance of what's happening. On the other hand, unless yours is to be a fairly unusual wedding, you won't have the normal resources of a voice-over commentary, graphic captions or an on-screen presenter, to help you tell the story and vary the treatment of the subject. In short, you'll be telling a totally familiar story and trying to make it entertaining, interesting and watchable entirely through the quality of your shooting, and your sound recording.

So let's spend a little time deciding what the basic approach should be, since your detailed planning is going to depend on that. You could treat the wedding as a production in its own right; going entirely for the ritual, the formal groups, the rehearsed set pieces. If you adopt this approach and all goes well, with no one tripping over or forgetting their lines, you may well end up with a programme as polished and glossy as a television commercial — and about as convincing. If this were the only view of the wedding we had there would be little to distinguish it from every other wedding, apart from the individual details of the church, the dresses, the faces and the setting for the reception.

A far better policy is to be sure to include all the important landmarks in the day's events — and to leaven the mixture with the unexpected and the spontaneous. Look for the human touches which reveal people as individuals. If the groom, waiting outside the church, asks the best man if he's got the ring, and the best man pats all his pockets pretending he's lost it, it's not exactly the most original joke in the world. But the interplay of expressions, especially if the best man is convincing enough for a glimmer of doubt to be seen crossing the groom's features, makes for a moment which is pure gold to the video producer. You can't plan for touches like this, but you need to be on the look-out for them, and be quick to capture them where they do occur.

Never play opposite children or animals, says an old showbusiness adage, the reason being that the unselfconscious appeal of either is difficult for even the most trained stage performer to match. So, if there are younger attendants and pages, keep an eye on them for the contrast between their sense of dignity and occasion when everyone's attention is on them, and their relaxed spontaneity at times when they're not under the spotlight. Children — and especially children closely involved with the wedding party itself — make a marvellous source of cutaways to bridge gaps in the action, or to link shots which would otherwise be difficult to match with a straight cut from one to the other.

The secret of shooting an event like a wedding which is not under your directorial control, is to think in sequences as you record your shots. Apart from specific linking shots which you can plan to a certain extent in advance (like the pan from the church clock to the cars arriving outside the gate), try to keep your shots brief and full of interest. Because you may set your camera up to cover a particular subject, and then find they take a long time to either move or to speak —or, indeed, do anything very much — this is difficult to guarantee unless you're able to edit in post-production. But if you are able to review your programme material and edit the best and most vivid shots together later, any gaps in the action can safely be taken care of then. On the other hand, tape is precious. If a promising subject lapses into inaction, look for something else and be prepared to come back to that subject when someone else has joined them, or an animated conversation has begun.

Gaps in the action

Don't forget two of video's particular strengths: people and movement form a combination which will help in spotting opportunities at any wedding. But whenever you have a subject which provides both, don't be tempted to linger too long. Seeing the bridesmaids struggling to arrange the bride's veil and train on a breezy day is an attractive image but, if the action goes on too long, look for a cutaway. Shoot a couple of seconds of a pageboy having his hair combed by a proud mother, and then you can cut back to the bridal party, either finishing their re-arrangements, or standing in line ready for the first of the photographs. Whatever the gap in the action, your cutaway will have covered it, and the audience won't be aware of any inconsistency.

Try to vary the angle and content of your shots as much as possible. In the previous example, if the bride and bridesmaids filled the frame as a three-shot, then look for a cutaway (like the page and his mother) which is a tightly framed two-shot, so the consecutive shots will cut together happily. If you don't want to go to a cutaway, but prefer to carry on with the action of your original shot, move position and shoot the action from a different angle — and with a different framing. This might mean a close-up of the bride's face, showing hands straightening her veil. Then you can cut back to a two-shot of the bridesmaids, before going back to your original position and framing for the end of the sequence.

If you stay with the bride and bridesmaids in this way, you'll need to watch the continuity between the shots if they're to cut together well. And you will still need a cutaway if you want to avoid having to follow them over to the setting for the photographs. Ideally the cutaway should link you visually to the next sequence, so one possibility might be a shot of the wedding photographer setting up his camera and starting to beckon people over. This will also give you the chance to shoot candid pictures of different guests and family members — which you can then re-edit into the wedding-photo sequence to inject a little pace and variety into what might otherwise be a slow and over-formal section of the programme. Another idea which is worth considering is to shoot occasional long shots with the background and many different groups of people in the frame, but showing insufficient detail to give rise to any continuity problems. These can then serve as stand-by cutaways, for solving any editing gap you didn't manage to cover on the day with a specific cutaway.

Keep a constant look-out for candid shots; where people are behaving spontaneously, and where they are unaware of your camera.

One helpful technique is to build up a rhythm, which helps keep track of the sequences as you compile them. Depending on the context within the overall order of events, try to mix specific shots relating to an arrival or a departure, part of the service, or one of the toasts at the reception, with more general shots of people relaxing and having a good time. So far as people are concerned, go for a mixture of the principal people involved — the bride and groom, bridesmaids and pages, best man and parents — with other friends, relatives and guests. But try to keep track of the faces you shoot; lavishing too much attention on a few photogenic faces, while ignoring others who may be closer or more important to the audience, won't earn you much in the way of appreciation. Any advice you can seek on this in advance, in terms of a must-shoot list, will be invaluable in ensuring you don't leave anyone out on the day.

Another point worth settling in advance is whether or not you want people to ignore the camera. In most cases, given the fly-on-the-wall approach we're aiming for, it's better if they don't see and react to your presence (although if you're a friend or relative of the couple, then it might be more difficult for people to accept you as part of the scenery). In that case, a briefing for the principals beforehand will probably be enough, as they're the people you most want to capture giving candid performances. If other friends and guests smile or wave at you in the beginning, the novelty will soon wear off and, in any case, these problems should only affect a small minority of shots. Most of the time they'll be far more concerned with the person they're talking to, or what's being said, or with the details of the ceremony and the speeches, to react to the presence of you and your camcorder.

All of which brings us to the threshold of producing the wedding video proper — the all-important planning and recce process, which can make the difference between an outstanding record of the day's events (and a more enjoyable day from your point of view in shooting it), and a disappointing struggle to keep up with a schedule which is slipping out of your control. With all the points covered in this chapter, and using the information contained in the first two chapters, you're now well enough acquainted with the problems and the priorities of shooting to approach the planning and recce with an insider's knowledge and experience. Until you know enough of what the job will involve, it's difficult to be sure you've asked all the right questions and remembered to check the most important points. Without these vital precautions, even the most detailed and pains-taking plans may contain a weakness which only becomes apparent — with possibly disastrous results — in the middle of the day itself.

Above all, don't be daunted by how complex the business seems with so much to take into consideration in your shooting. The point is that by reviewing all these possibilities at the pre-planning stage, you're going a long way towards eliminating them as risks when the shooting begins. From this point onwards, your planning will be much more detailed — and more specifically related to *this* couple, *this* wedding, *this* church and *this* reception on *this* particular day. From here to the end of the programme you will be dealing more often with real priorities and real op-portunities, and less with general considerations which may or may not apply to your particular wedding video.

Planning and Reconnaissance — the Church

Now we're moving from the general to the particular — from the factors which have to be taken into account with all approaches to wedding-video production, to the making of a specific programme. It's time to begin making some decisions. Start by going back to the couple at the centre of the whole event, and discuss with them what you should try to put into the programme; from the pictures of their childhood and adolescence, right through to the most appropriate scene on which to end the programme.

Now, above all, is the time to foresee any potential snags, particularly conflicts of time or place, which may put you in danger of missing something more important through being delayed in traffic or trying to find a parking place. For example, we mentioned earlier the possibility of including a sequence of the bride and her party getting ready at the house before leaving for the church. It's a good idea, from several points of view, in that it instils a note of spontaneity and humanity before we reach the formal sections of the programme, and it helps to heighten the drama and sense of occasion that a good wedding video should have. But think carefully first. If you shoot this as it happens, then you almost certainly have to end on the bride leaving with her father to start her journey to the church. If you're lucky, and if you arrange with the driver to take a slightly roundabout route, you can actually reach the church in time to shoot their arrival. But you'll miss the arrival of the groom, the best man, the ushers and the guests — and, because you will have to work that much harder to do them justice in the rest of the programme, you may miss something else, and so on.

Planning the opening sequence

It would be better by far to start with a compromise. We said in the previous chapter that your ideal role on the day is that of a camera-equipped fly on the wall rather than a television director, so you should react to events rather than try to control them. In this case, however, all the problems can be solved by considering tampering just once with reality. Ask the bride and her family if it's possible to shoot them getting ready on the day before the wedding. It may not have quite the same edge as it would on the day itself, with all of the additional tension of having to meet a timetable which is already running, but that too could be an advantage. People won't be so tense that they might overreact to the presence of you and your camera. (But don't be too surprised if the bride objects to this idea, because she will always know it was a staged, rather than a 'real', event.)

The end of the opening sequence: the bride prepares to leave for the church (left), and walks out past the camera on her father's arm (right) — and it's all being shot the day before!

You'll also have to decide what details your clients want to see recorded. Does the styling of the bride's hair qualify for inclusion, and can you set that up on the day before — sufficiently to include it as a sequence in your shooting — so as not to interfere with preparations on the day itself? What about the

bride having her face made up, and her father struggling into his best suit, or the hired morning coat? What about the bridesmaids and the bride's mother, and any pages and attendants who may be supposed to leave from the same house?

If you are able to shoot this section the day before, you also need to think about how it should end. The chances are you won't be able to shoot everybody getting into their cars as if they're driving off to the church, so you'll have to consider how else you can suggest departure and link into the shots you'll shoot of them all arriving at the church on the actual day of the wedding. One option would be to shoot the sequence from the bride's point of view, which is not only logical as it is above all her day (or at least tomorrow will be!), but it also provides the opportunity to suggest their departure for the church as, one by one they leave the room in which they've all been getting ready. The very last shot in this sequence could be the bride's father coming to tell her that the car's arrived and it's time to go, and, as they go through the door into the hall, you can cut (in the edited programme) back to the events at the church.

Shooting this section on the previous day creates one additional possibility. You can always shoot some material at the groom's house, showing him and his best man and their immediate guests getting ready too, so that you could intercut the two sequences at the very beginning. This gives you two advantages: apart from the symmetry of the arrangement, the whole idea of two sequences running in parallel provides you with instant cutaways, simply through cutting from one to the other, and back again, in the final edit.

Beware of one restriction though. For the timetable to be convincing, you will have to show that the groom and best man are ready well before the bride. This is chiefly a matter of the way in which you edit the finished sequences, but it also governs the amount of material you need to shoot at each of the two locations. In the finished programme, you can then show the groom and best man arriving at the church before the guests. And you can still continue cutting backwards and forwards between the guests assembling at the church and the last, rushed preparations before the bridal party actually leaves (shot, as explained, on the day before).

It's also worth making a note (since you are shooting a day in advance and the whole thing will be done again in earnest a day later) of any potential problems over continuity. Clothes shouldn't be as much of a problem as they might otherwise be, since wedding clothes offer less opportunity for variation between one day and the next. But it's still possible for the best man, for example, to wear a different tie on the day if the rule is lounge suits rather than morning coats. So be sure to check.

Recceing the locations

If you and the couple decide that one or both of these preparation sequences are to be included in the programme, you also need to recce the locations to identify any snags or shooting opportunities. Check the rooms where people will be getting ready. Are they dark enough to need lighting specially and, if so, how little extra lighting can you get away with? Since this is one area where the event is being staged for your benefit, extra lighting won't be as obtrusive as it would be during the wedding proper (and we'll come to that later). But it's still worth keeping it to a minimum to save time and effort when you shoot, and to allow you to concentrate on what you are seeing in the viewfinder. If you do decide lights are needed, check access to power sockets, what kinds of adaptors and extension leads will be needed, and which of the sockets are likely to be in use for other purposes when you come to shoot the sequence.

Watch out for limitations imposed by the physical size of the rooms. Can you move far enough back from your subject to capture him or her in the lens? If you move some of the furniture, can you win yourself some extra space by shooting from the hall or landing through the open door? If the location is a bungalow, or a ground-floor flat, or if you're able to arrange for some of the action to take place in a downstairs room of the house, then consider the possibility of shooting the interior scene through an open window, keeping the framing tight enough to disguise the fact you're not inside.

If you're going to shoot at both houses (bride's family and groom's family), then look for differences which help the audience realise, without having to explain to it, that different shots with different people in them are actually being taken in two different places. If one has modern furniture, for example, then make a note to feature it in the background of some of the establishing shots. And if the other has heavier antique furniture, or a different style of decor, then carefully chosen shots can ensure the audience isn't unnecessarily confused when you switch between one location and the other. If the furniture is similar in both places, then look for individual pictures and ornaments to establish the identity of the setting.

It's time to move on now to the most critical phase of all in the planning and recce procedure — to the church, chapel or registry office where the ceremony will take place. There are two reasons why you need to check the location out very carefully, but the first, and most important, is to make contact with the minister or official who will actually perform the ceremony. Unless you have permission, you may well not even be allowed across the threshold with your camera and equipment. So you need to make contact as early as possible in the planning of your programme, to find out what the official reaction to your request to record the wedding is likely to be.

Attitudes vary very much. In some cases, priests and officials alike are perfectly happy for you to enter the church or the registry office to make your recording, as they realise the pleasure which a well-made wedding video can offer to the couple and their families in the years to come. Others have suffered at the hands of the camcorder cowboys — amateur or semi-professional — who have proved to be an all-too-intrusive presence in what should still be a sober and formal ceremony. They remember all too well the batteries of lights around the walls, the lamps shone in people's faces, the cables everywhere, the constant shifting from place to place during the service, and the occasional request to repeat some of the responses so they can shoot them from a different angle, or because the sound wasn't quite right.

It's your job, in cases like this, to allay doubts and worries by explaining that you will be happy to follow whatever rules the minister chooses to impose. In some cases it won't be his decision anyway, as it may depend on policy laid down by the parish council or some other regulatory body. Whatever the situation you meet, one thing is certain — it's far better to ensure the vicar, priest or registrar is on your side, as his or her co-operation can make all the difference to the success of your programme. So be as reassuring as you can. Explain that you will respect the sanctity of the location and the importance of the

The two most likely camera positions inside the church — alongside the couple or, the second-best option, at the back end of the aisle.

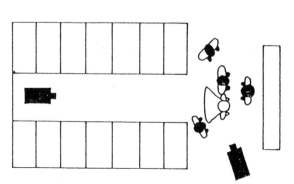

ceremony. Underline the fact that you will work within the rules, once you know what those are, and that you would be happier if they could be agreed in advance, to avoid any misunderstandings.

Recording the ceremony

The end result of these conversations should be an agreement to one of four methods of recording the actual ceremony. You may be given the go-ahead to shoot from a position at the front of the church or registry office, or secondly, from a position at the back of the building, looking at the couple over the heads of the assembled guests. Thirdly, you may not be allowed to shoot inside the building at all, but be limited to recording the sounds of the service on an audio recorder. Finally, and most limiting of all, you may not even be allowed inside to record an audio track of the wedding ceremony — which does create certain problems.

We'll deal with all these different cases, starting with the ideal situation where you can choose your camera position for yourself. There's no single place which fulfils all the requirements, but there's little doubt the best compromise involves setting up the shoot from the right-hand side of the church (if you're facing the altar), slightly in front of the bride and groom as they stand in front of the minister. That gives you an equal opportunity for three-shots of the couple and the minister, and close-ups of any of the three to accord with what is being said at the time. Bear in mind that the couple will almost certainly want to have the vows recorded in full, together with the minister's pronouncement that they are now husband and wife at the conclusion of the ceremony, so you will have to keep the camera running for the whole of that part of the proceedings. Don't forget to ask how long different stages are likely to take, so you can make sure that batteries and tapes won't run out at this most vital section of the service.

Two other problems need to be thought about well in advance of the actual shoot, and these are sound and lights. To your clients, the soundtrack of the video is almost as important as the pictures; they don't just want to see themselves making their vows, they will want to hear them as well. So you need to be prepared to be able to pick up good, clear sound in a building which presents you with a difficult acoustic challenge. The echoes and reverberations within a stone church form a complex mixture of sounds, to which your camera microphone responds quite differently from your own ears. Voices nearby may well

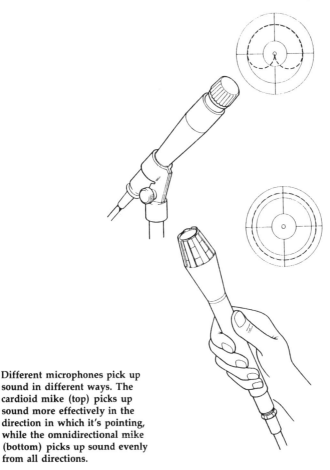

Different microphones pick up sound in different ways. The cardioid mike (top) picks up sound more effectively in the direction in which it's pointing, while the omnidirectional mike (bottom) picks up sound evenly from all directions.

be overwhelmed by echoes and footsteps, and other extraneous noises reflected from the far end of the building. The real solution to this is to have a separate microphone for recording the voices. At its most sophisticated, this might involve the groom wearing a miniature radio mike on his lapel, so that you can pick up the voices of the minister and the couple without the need for trailing cables. Because your mike is so close to the sound you want to record, other noises shouldn't cause any problem. It also leaves you free to use the camera microphone to pick up general atmospheric sound — once you have made sure that connecting a second mike to your camera doesn't switch off the normal camera-mike circuit. If it does, you will have to use two microphones connected to an audio mixer, the output of which is connected to the auxiliary microphone socket on the camcorder.

Radio microphones tend to be expensive, although they can be hired by the day from specialist suppliers. You can also hide an ordinary cable mike close to the couple and the minister, but be careful the cable doesn't show up in any of your shots, that the microphone is placed so it picks up the three principal voices equally and, perhaps most important of all, that there is absolutely no chance of anyone tripping over the cable.

Another problem with some church interiors is that they tend to be dark, so you have to face the question of whether some form of background lighting is needed. Today's cameras are so good at shooting in poor light conditions that you may well be able to manage without any extra lighting at all. This is much the best course of action if you find the ambient light inside the church is adequate, but the only way you can be completely sure is to ask permission to shoot someone at various points around the church on your recce visit, and then to examine the resulting footage carefully.

Is what you see a recognisable and individual figure, or a dark, mysterious silhouette? Can you see the shape and details of the face, the colours and textures of the clothes? Sometimes a sharp contrast between light and dark on different sides of the face can be extremely dramatic — an effect that painters call 'chiaroscuro' — but with moving pictures this can cause problems whenever the subject moves relative to the dividing line between bright light and dark shade.

If the lighting is uniformly subdued, another possibility is to use the low-light facility provided on some of the more sophisticated, semi-professional cameras. But since these compensate for the low levels of light entering the lens by turning up the gain of the camera's internal amplifiers, the noise in the picture is increased too. The result is that the picture seems brighter, but there will be a 'grainy' effect caused by the higher level of background noise in the electronic signals which the camera is recording on the tape. Once again, the only way to see whether or not the compromise is acceptable is to try out the camera beforehand — put someone in position inside the church, shoot some material from different angles, and then play it back over your VCR so you can see it on the television screen in the same way as your audience will be watching the end result.

Background lighting

If, after your recce, you do decide the lighting has to be boosted artificially, you then have a series of problems of a different kind to solve. The first one is, will the minister allow lighting in the church in the first place? If he will allow you to put up lights, where should you put them, and when? Check the sockets fitted in the church — in many older buildings round-pin sockets are still used, and you may need to track down an appropriate adaptor. The location of the sockets may call for long extension leads so the lights may be placed where you want them; where they will provide maximum effect and minimum distraction on the day itself. The timetable of other weddings is absolutely critical. You need enough time between the previous wedding and the one you're filming to allow you to gain access to the church, set up your lights and microphones and then to move back outside in time to cover the action sequences of the guests arriving.

What kind of lights will you need? Essentially, we're talking about background lighting — floods rather than spots — to lift the general light level inside the church without aiming at any specific targets. There are two reasons for this. Lighting the interior in general gives you the maximum choice of subjects while covering the key sections of the ceremony. If you light specific areas of the church, you're automatically limiting yourself to fewer subjects as the ceremony continues, since the contrast between the lit areas and the unlit sections of the church would be unacceptably sharp. Secondly, any of the guests who are placed in the areas of bright light are going to be distracted as they will feel, literally, that they're in the spotlight. If you light the bride, as one of the principal figures in the ceremony, the chances are, if she is in a white dress, that it will reflect the light so intensely that the background will be overshadowed completely. On the other hand, if you can keep your lighting spread out evenly over the whole interior, it will become accepted as part of the background.

Sometimes you may find that the church isn't uniformly dark, but offers patches which are quite well lit and other patches which are in deep shadow. If this is the case, you need to place your lights to lift the brightness of the shadowed areas to give you the maximum range of subjects. Don't try to make them too bright so they outshine the well-lit areas — by keeping them slightly darker, you will maintain plenty of depth in the background to your pictures. Your audience will expect churches to have dark corners. All you're trying to do is light the picture so that it appears, through the camera, just like the unlit church would to the human eye.

The ideal lighting kit for this kind of requirement is made up of two or three quartz video lights, preferably of the relatively low-power type, called 'redheads' by the professionals. They should be fitted with adjustable shutters, called 'barn doors', to allow you to screen the beam so the light doesn't shine into the camera or into the faces of the congregation. The trick is to place them carefully, so they light as much as possible of the critically dark areas within your field of view, without shining into anyone's eyes, or without the lights themselves appearing within your frame at any time.

Video lights have an adjustable control at the back which allows you to focus the beam to a narrow spot, or to widen it to a flood effect. The flood option is what's needed here, although you will usually find that the trick method of producing a soft background illumination, by bouncing the beam off the ceiling, won't work. The roofs of most churches are too high and too dark to reflect anything worthwhile, so you have to look for other reflective surfaces to help spread the effect of your lights, without producing distractingly over-bright areas in your picture.

One final problem worth bearing in mind is the effect of the lights you use on the colour temperature of the scene you will be shooting. If the light which is available inside the church is provided by daylight filtering in through the windows and doorways, the artificial light you are adding to the background of the picture is going to upset the balance.

You have two options here. You can compromise by setting the camera to a daylight balance — this will give the people a warm, softly yellow cast which is preferable to the daylight-looking blue which would be achieved if you set the white balance to match the video lights. The other option is to fit a daylight filter to each of your lights. This will reduce the output slightly, but setting your white balance to daylight in these circumstances should secure you a perfectly balanced picture.

What can you do if you find that lights are out of the question? Be sure to choose your shots, your subjects and your framing very carefully. On your recce, make a special point of looking for any areas which are better illuminated than others, and make a note of them.

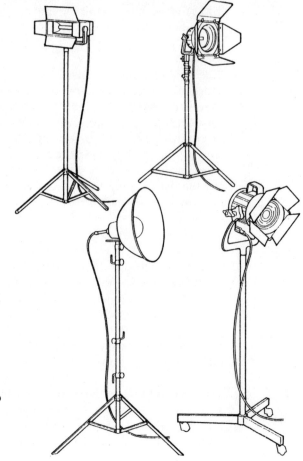

Some of the types of lights available — best are the medium-power spots, called redheads (top right), with 'barn doors' to deflect the beam exactly where you want it.

Remember that your camera will pick up more light at the wider end of the zoom, so try to limit yourself to angles and subjects which make the most of these wider shots, in parts of the church where the light level is higher than average.

Shooting from the back of the church

All of the above has been based on the supposition that you have virtually unrestricted access to the church for the ceremony. But what will happen if the minister says you can only shoot from the back of the church? This will restrict the range and types of shot you can record, but it's still possible to record something of the ceremony with a little pre-planning. First of all, check that it will still be possible to record the sounds of the ceremony, with one or more microphones placed close enough to the altar to pick up the ritual and the responses. If so, then you will need longer leads to link to the microphones from the back of the church, and you'll need to double-check, on your recce visit, the exact position(s) from which the mike(s) will give you good clear sound and an even balance between the voices. It's even more important again to find places where the microphones can't be knocked over by accident. If they are, you'll lose the sound and not be able to do anything about it from your camera position at the back of the church.

Like so many of the details associated with wedding videos, most of these problems become less daunting with experience. A good way for the beginner to test out skills like the correct combination and placement of microphones, is to ask permission to practise during the wedding rehearsal. Be careful to be as quiet and as unobtrusive as possible. Too much of your presence made obvious at the rehearsal may mean a total ban on the day itself.

The main advantage of setting up microphones and cables at the rehearsal is that it allows you to try out mike positions and recording levels with the people and the acoustics as they will be on the day. Because you're concentrating on close-up recording of the minister and the couple, the presence or absence of all the guests will make little difference. The camera mike will pick up the general atmosphere in the church on the wedding day proper and, unlike the individual mikes, that will be under your control throughout.

But the voices of your three principals are vitally important. Different people speak at different volumes — especially when under stress, as they may well be with the excitement and tension of the occasion, and the need to concentrate on the words which they have to repeat. This added drama may make them speak more quietly than usual, or it may encourage them to speak more loudly and emphasise the words. Either way, you will need time to experiment with different microphone positions and settings, and the rehearsal should allow you to do this to the point where you have one less problem to worry about when you record the wedding itself.

So far as your actual camera position at the back of the church is concerned, try to make the most of what is available. In order to cover the key points in the ceremony, you'll need to be able to frame the best view you can of the bride and the groom with the minister. If you are able to position yourself at the far end of the aisle, you should be able to zoom in to shoot the backs of the couple with the minister behind them — not ideal, admittedly, but similar to the view enjoyed by those guests placed near the back of the church. In order to hold this view for long enough to capture the responses you'll need a tripod to steady the camcorder, so you will need to ensure you have room for this to be placed where it cannot be kicked by people passing, or present a trap for the unwary on their way into or out of the church.

Another shot which you can possibly capture from the back of the church — but one which would be impossible from the favoured camera position next to the groom and the best man at the front — is that of the bride and her father entering the church as the wedding is about to begin. This needs careful planning, however, as you need to avoid catching them against the bright daylight outside, or they will fade into dark and threatening silhouettes and give entirely the wrong impression of the scene you are shooting. Try to find a position which, while allowing you to capture the group at the altar in long shot, will also allow you to turn to shoot the bride and her father coming in through the door — against the background of the interior of the porch, rather than the outside. This less brightly illuminated background will not produce so harsh a contrast, allowing your camera to capture the detail of the two figures on their way into the church, moments before the ceremony begins.

This last shot is another one which it would be wise to try out in advance, by shooting it at the rehearsal. If you can secure the co-operation of the bride and her father, and the permission of the minister, you can see whether or not a shot which may be attractive in theory, will actually work in practice. If there are problems, it may also be possible to improve the look of the shot by placing a lamp inside the porch to increase the overall illumination. Again, this should be with the approval of all concerned, and a lot of care should be taken over the location of the light so the projecting legs of its supporting tripod can't pose a hazard to anyone entering or leaving the church. Nor, through the lamp being knocked over at the vital moment, should its position threaten the successful outcome of the intended shot.

Depending on the routine of the ceremony, the layout of the church and the wishes of the couple, you also need to decide whether or not you want to record the bride and groom leaving the church at the conclusion of the ceremony — after signing the register — whether you need to shoot the actual signing itself, or whether to use the time to set up outside ready for the official photographs to be taken. If it's not the intention to cover the signing of the register, one useful option is to stay in position at the back of the church and wait for the bride and groom to re-emerge, so this time you can shoot them walking down the aisle towards you, and end when they walk out of the church doorway.

This is another advantage of being placed at the back of the church. However, if you are initially positioned at the front, it might be possible to change positions and move to the back of the church while the register is being signed. Once again check with the minister and the couple, and try out both locations during the rehearsal. Finally, don't forget that, if you intend to shoot the bride and groom walking out of the church, you need to follow them fairly closely so as to be in position when the photography begins, without actually getting in the way of the official photographer.

Sound-only coverage

What happens if the minister won't allow cameras inside the church at all? Here you have a problem of a different kind. In a way, this presents you with a much simpler task inside the church, in that you can set up a tape recorder to capture the whole of the service, if need be, without having to worry about the camcorder tape and battery life, lights and camera positions, or framing. Instead, you will have to consider some different problems. For example, if you are recording the ceremony on an audio tape recorder, have you arrangements for copying that tape onto the audio tracks of your video cassette at the post-production stage? If you still intend to use several different microphones, you need to check the same points as before. Where do the microphones go, what settings do you use for recording voices and atmosphere, where do you place the recorder itself, and who will operate it? You have two options here. The first is that you can switch from being a camera operator to working as a sound engineer for the duration of the service. This will leave you free to concentrate on the objective of capturing the ceremony on sound as clearly as you can, but you will have to plan the point at which you need to move out of the church, at the end of the ceremony, and set up to resume the video shoot in time to capture the taking of the official photographs. It also means you won't be able to shoot suitable cut-aways outside to cover the sounds of the ceremony on the finished programme. These will have to be done some other time.

The second option is to find someone else who can be relied on to record a good soundtrack. Go through the details of what you want them to do, show them the recording equipment and take them through the drill — a good idea would be to bring them along to the rehearsal and put them through their paces with the recorder to see what kind of results they can deliver. If all goes well, you have one less worry. If problems come to light, you have a chance to correct them before the day of the wedding itself.

This now leaves you free to shoot outside while the ceremony is in progress. We'll look at the question of covering shots for the audio track in more detail in a later chapter, but for the time being it's worth incorporating in your plan any exterior cutaways of the church which could be shot at this point in the day, and which would be useful in building up a more varied and ambitious sequence at the post-production stage. For now, all you need do is look for suitable subjects and framings; for example, the church doorway, the tower or spire, the noticeboard, the porch, the windows, different views of the building itself, the gate from the road outside and the path up to the porch. If there are any unusual features specific to this building — from oddly shaped gargoyles to intricately carved stonework — now is the time to make a note of them. It might also be worth shooting some of them if you have time, although you should be careful of continuity problems. If your recce takes place on a dull day, and the wedding in brilliant sunshine, then some of your recce shots may be wasted. But if they do match, they'll save you valuable time on what is likely to be a very busy day.

A video without the wedding ceremony

Finally, we need to consider how to cope with the minister who won't allow any recording at all within the portals of his church. Statistically, this is perhaps the least likely response you will meet to your request for permission to shoot the wedding but, if it happens, you need to have a contingency plan which takes this option into account. First of all, you could try to reassure the minister, by the means described earlier, of your respect for the church as a location — and for the importance of the wedding ceremony itself. You need to underline your willingness to adhere strictly to any rules that might be imposed as a condition of your being able to shoot within the church, or record the ceremony on audio tape. If all this persuasion and reassurance fails to negotiate a lifting of the ban, what can you do?

In a sense, it suggests a production of *Hamlet* without the Prince — a wedding video without the wedding. But remember, the basic purpose of the video is to provide a moving-pictures-and-sound version of the classic wedding album. Until very recently, it was rare indeed for albums to include any photographs at all of the ceremony itself. Couples had to be content with photographs of their arrival at the church, the formal pictures outside after the ceremony, and shots of themselves and their guests at the reception — and, indeed, some couples still prefer this. So if your video programme has to cover the same ground, the scenes you *can* shoot will still provide endless pleasure to those involved, even without the ceremony itself. But you need to find some way of bridging the gap, before moving on to the reception and the rest of the day.

Planning and Reconnaissance — the Reception

Now it's time to move on to the social and celebratory part of the wedding, after the ritual of the ceremony itself. Here the emphasis is completely different, as are the problems you will face in trying to capture it on video. On the one hand, there will be no problem about gaining access to the location to prepare and to shoot the proceedings; on the other hand, these proceedings are likely to be less formal than the routine in the church, so your planning and your research have to try and reduce the unknown and unpredictable factors to a minimum.

Before we leave the church, however, let's look at a couple more possibilities for creative shooting. We've explained earlier about the usefulness of using the official photographer as a director for your shooting — capturing his efforts to marshal people into groups, along with the formal groups themselves as he's photographing them and the more relaxed, less posed shots of the remaining guests watching the photographs being taken. Now, however, you need to be aware of the possibility of the photographic session serving your purpose in another way altogether — acting, in effect, as a delaying tactic.

It all depends on whether the bride and groom want you to shoot them leaving for the reception, or arriving at the reception, or both. If it's both, then you have to enlist their aid, together with that of the driver of their car, the drivers of the other hired cars, and a member of the family to look after the guests. The object of all this is to delay the journey from the church to the reception long enough to allow you to

A classic dilemma — usually it's better to go for the rush and movement of the couple's dash to the car, from the church than leave early to shoot their relatively low-key arrival at the reception.

pack away your equipment, drive to the reception ahead of anyone else, park your car, unload the kit and set up ready to shoot the arrival of the bride and groom, followed by the rest of the party.

The first essential is to know how much delay to ask for. So part of your recce should involve packing away all your recording equipment at the church, driving to the venue booked for the reception by the shortest and quickest route, and unloading and setting up ready for the arrival of the cars. Add on ten minutes to allow for extra parking problems on the day, and you know what kind of instructions to give the drivers, and to the person who's going to make sure the guests delay their departure by a similar amount.

Of course, all this pre-planning won't be necessary if you don't need to shoot the bride and groom departing *and* arriving. If it's a straight choice between one sequence and the other, you may be able to take your chance along with the rest of the party — but it's still a good idea to have some arrangement with the reception venue to reserve a parking space for you. This way you won't miss vital minutes trying to find a place to leave your car, and then have to carry your equipment a long way from the parking space to the reception room.

If the choice is left up to you, which is the better alternative? Do you shoot the bride and groom leaving the church, and then cut to them already at the reception, or do you leave them amid the formal photographs at the church, to allow you to be in position ready for their arrival at the hotel? Much will depend on the locations and the details in their own wedding plan but, in general, the dash for the bridal car, with all the well-wishers cheering and throwing confetti, is a much more worthwhile shot than seeing them arrive at the reception and then waiting for all the others to follow. That's bound to provide an unwelcome pause in the action, and to use time which could have been better spent at the church, rounding off that section of the programme properly.

Making the most of the unusual

There *will* be exceptions to that rule, for a variety of reasons. One of these might be the location for the reception itself. If there is anything unusual or spectacular about it, then showing the bride and groom arriving there is a good way of springing a surprise on anyone seeing the tape for the first time (anyone who wasn't at the wedding — your secondary audience, if you like). Such is the pressure of advance bookings on successful hotels and restaurants, and so familiar the routine, that more and more couples are looking for somewhere unusual to hold the reception. Even some riverboats, or steam trains on preserved railways, now offer a full wedding-reception service, and there's little doubt that seeing the old well-worn succession of toasts and speeches taking place afloat, or in the dining car of a moving train, does add a powerful dash of the unexpected to an otherwise welcome but predictable part of the day.

If this is the case then, as a video producer, it's up to you to make the most of it. Try to recce the location as thoroughly as possible, even though, when you visit it in advance, you'll have to use even more imagination to visualise the scene on the day itself. It's likely that boats, trains or any other unusual location will be heavily involved with ordinary traffic on most days when you can carry out the recce. So far, wedding receptions will be something of a sideline for them, so you'll have to push your way through the crowds and try to check out the camera angles and framings, the possibilities for cutaways and the way your bridal party will approach the location on the day of your shoot.

It's impossible to lay down rules, since these locations will differ even more sharply from one another than hotels and restaurants. However, if a location is really unusual, one attractive option is to reveal it as part of a linking shot. Let's assume the reception is to take place on a train, or a river steamer. Try and pick a camera position looking at the spot where the bridal car will draw up at the end of its drive from the church — without revealing any sign in the framing of the shot that there is anything unusual about the location. Although it's a parking space alongside a landing stage, or at a station entrance, by carefully positioning your camera you can make it look like a car-parking spot outside a perfectly ordinary hotel or restaurant. If you then imagine the car drawing up (and, to make the most of a shot like this, you might need to tell the driver of the bridal car *exactly* where to pull up on the day), you need to visualise the bride and groom climbing out and walking towards the edge of your frame. Of course, what you will do in the event is pan with them to reveal the fact that they're nowhere near the kind of hotel or restaurant everyone will be expecting, but that they're climbing aboard a train or steamer.

This type of shot gives you a really stylish link between the routine at the church and the surprise of the reception, one which you can follow up during the speeches, the toasts and the meal by picking out unusual cutaways to remind your audience of where all this is taking place. Riverside scenery seen through the portholes of the steamer, life-belts, the steersman at the wheel, pauses to progress through the locks, or to avoid other traffic — all these need to be noted on your recce so you can plan to use them when you want to on the actual day, without having to wait for inspiration to strike when most urgently needed.

Linking to the reception

Of course receptions like these are still out of the ordinary. Let's return now to the more familiar and more conventional reception, and how to do the event justice by careful pre-planning. We left our couple when they were *en route* from the church, having been captured leaving, closely followed by you, your assistant (if you have one) and your video equipment. Find out before your recce what the routine is going to be, so far as the guests are concerned. As they arrive at the reception, will they be greeted by members of the hotel and restaurant staff, who will take their coats and offer them a drink (leaving them free to wander through to the room where the meal is to be served — or the garden, if there is one, and if the weather is fine and warm on the day), or will they be met by the bride and groom, their respective parents, the best man and the bridesmaids, in a receiving line? This is becoming more common today, and its advantage from your point of view is that it offers you two valuable opportunities; it provides a focus on which you can start your coverage of the reception, and it also offers a chance to shoot a comprehensive selection of individuals from among the guests as they arrive and pass along the receiving line.

For the present, though, all you need to know is — if there is to be a receiving line — where they will stand, where the guests will move to join the line, and which way they will move when they leave it. You will need at least two camera positions: one looking at the line from the arriving guests' point of view, so that your audience can see where everyone is standing and where the guests will move on to once they've met everyone in the line. This is effectively your establishing shot for this section of the programme.

A bird's-eye view of the receiving line, showing the two best camera positions for capturing a variety of material.

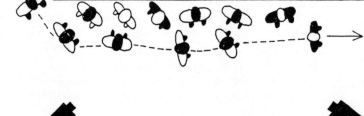

You then need to find a position where you can shoot several different angles and framings of different people being greeted by the various members of the receiving line — without any danger to you of getting in the way, becoming a distraction, or being denied a clear view of what's happening. At this stage it's a matter of having to use your imagination. But you can check positions and distances, which won't change between your recce and the day of the wedding, and you can also use your camera to check out the levels of available light. As the reception is more under your control, or, more exactly, that of your clients, it might even be possible to move the position of the receiving line slightly — if by doing so it avoids a particularly dark part of an otherwise well-lit room, or if it frees you from the problem of a window behind the line turning it, and the guests, into a series of silhouettes. Wherever possible, try to cover this part of the reception without using extra lights. Apart from their inhibiting effect on what should be an entirely spontaneous moment, the need to set them up and then move them afterwards will severely hamper your ability to keep up with events and will cause a distraction.

Short and simple links

There are other ways of bridging the gap, in time and place, between the church and the reception, and this too is something which should be on your list of targets for the reception reconnaissance. Sometimes it's possible to cut straight from the scene outside the church, with the photographs still being taken or the bride and groom having been sent off by their guests, to the reception almost in full swing. What's needed is a visual device which can sum up the change of place and the passing of time in a single cut, and an ideal example — as mentioned earlier — is a pair of clocks. Let's imagine for a moment that our church is one of those with a clock in the tower. If you're able to position yourself for your final shot of the bride and groom leaving the church so that you can tilt the camera upwards to end on the clock, then half your problem is solved.

Of course, making the shot work properly may mean compromising over your ideal camera position. For example, you may need to be outside the church gate next to the car to get the best transition, and you may need, once again, to employ the driver's help over exactly where and at what angle to the church he brings the car to a stop. It also means you won't be able to end the shot on the car taking off down the road, unless you structure the sequence differently and plan your camera position accordingly. You could, for instance, shoot the couple rushing into the car in showers of confetti, then move quickly to stand behind, and slightly to one side of, the car, which allows you to pick out the clock and pan and tilt down to reveal the car accelerating away down the road.

Whichever alternative you try, planning the sequence and the camera positions will have to be done as part of your recce at the church. But the reason we're discussing it now is that you will only know whether the church sequence is likely to work when you've checked out the reception part of the link. In an ideal world, you'll find a clock somewhere which you can use as the other half of your link. A clock on the wall behind the table seating the couple and their families would be perfect. A clock on a side table, even a carriage clock or an antique clock among the wedding presents (if these are on display) would serve, as would one visible from the receiving line. If any of these options are available you know the link will work — but you will have to find a camera position which will allow you to incorporate your clock into the opening shot of the reception sequence.

If not, then see if it's possible to cheat a little. It might even be feasible to have a clock moved into the reception room purposely, or you could explore the possibilities of having one of the hotel staff look at his or her watch — remember to shoot the watch in close-up — and then signal as if to order the waiters and waitresses to bring in the food and drinks. By cutting to the reception as drinks or plates of food are being brought in, the link is smoothly established for once and for all.

That's one example of a visual link between church and reception. There are other ways of achieving that same objective smoothly and economically, in terms of time, and shooting effort. For example, flowers in the borders at the church, and flowers on the table at the reception, would make a useful link, but once again your shooting has to be planned accordingly. Reverting to the scene of the departure from the church, you need to bring flowers, in close-up, into your closing shot. One useful option here would be to end on a change-focus shot between the bride and groom's car driving away in the background, and a mass of colourful flowers in the foreground.

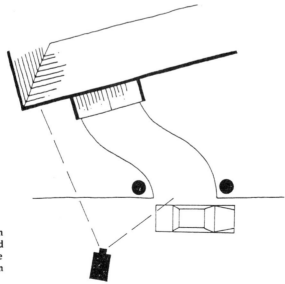

A bird's-eye view of the best position for capturing the couple emerging from the church and leaving for the reception — in a single shot.

Shift focus between background and foreground so that you end on the flowers, and then cut straight to the flowers, also in close-up, at the reception, before pulling out to show the event in full swing.

Once again, you may not know about flowers, and where they'll be placed at the reception, while you carry out your recce, but bear the possibility in mind and discuss it with the bride. If the flowers which are present on the day turn out not to be in the right place for your purposes, then be ready to move them to make your shot possible. And if flowers will not work as the linking device, be ready to think of something else. A cutaway from the shot of the bride and groom driving away from the church to one of the individuals among the watching guests, followed by a cut to that same guest in the very different surroundings of the reception, could make the point of the change of location very briefly and economically.

Recceing the reception

Now let's turn to the reception as an event. What should your sense of priorities be in planning and recceing its coverage? The reception has two main purposes from your point of view — it provides another opportunity for candid and informal shots of bride, groom, friends, family and guests, relaxing once the formal part of the wedding is over; and it also provides a framework for recording the speeches and toasts which serve as the basis for all kinds of memories of the day in the months and years to come. But how you plan to achieve those objectives depends on the kind of reception which has been organised.

So begin with a series of questions to determine what will happen after everyone arrives on the day. We'll assume that we now know whether a receiving line is part of the plan. But, whether it is or not, what is scheduled to happen next? Will the guests be left free to meet friends and be introduced to new acquaintances over a glass or two, before moving into the dining room to sit down for the meal and speeches? If so, will this take place indoors or outside? Be careful to look at both locations, so that you're fully prepared for whatever the weather may send on the day. What kind of service will be involved for the meal itself? Will waiters and waitresses bring it in, course by course, or will it be a help-yourself buffet, with the guests only sitting down to eat and to listen to the speeches? Apart from the table with the couple and their respective families, will they be sitting down according to a pre-set plan which may help you target individuals who will definitely need to be included, or will they be left to choose their own tables, with their own friends, or members of their own families?

Whatever the planned routine, you will need to schedule your shooting accordingly. Generally speaking, a buffet gives you greater freedom to move around to record varied shots of the guests, and of the bride and groom greeting individuals among the throng. In any case, shooting people choosing food and having it put on their plates will probably produce better and more varied pictures than shots of them being served at the table. So far as the meal itself is concerned, you're looking for a brief, but varied, sequence to cover the serving and the eating of the food, to bring us to the essential part of the reception — the toasts and the speeches.

Shooting the speeches is another area where routine will come to your aid to a certain extent. Tradition dictates the main toasts — to the bride and groom, to the bridesmaids, to the bride's parents, and so on — together with who makes each speech to introduce the proposal of the toast, and the order in which these are delivered. But there are variations, and you need to check with the couple whether there will be any other additional speeches, or changes to the routine ones, which need to be taken into account. You also need to check with them, at the earliest possible opportunity, whether they want all of the speeches recorded in full, or whether they want just highlights included in the finished programme.

This is where you need to do some research. If you have the chance to talk to the principal speakers —the groom, the bride's father, the best man, and so on — to find out roughly what they're going to say and, more importantly, how long they expect to take to say it, you'll be well on the way to being able to decide how to cover this stage of the reception. Ideally, it should be possible to cover the speeches in their entirety. If the average speech is around three minutes in length, this would give you a total of ten to 12 minutes for this part of the reception — which, in the context of around an hour and a quarter for the complete programme (as we discussed in an earlier chapter), would give a reasonable balance.

Covering the speeches in full requires some more careful planning. The first priority is how to record good quality sound, so the speeches themselves can be heard clearly when the programme is played back. As with the responses in the church, you need to consider how to record both the speeches and the general atmosphere in the room to provide a more lifelike combination. If you pick a camera position somewhere to one side of the room, this will allow you to shoot both the speakers and the people listening to the speech and responding to the toasts. It will also allow you to use the camera microphone to record the general atmosphere — the subdued hum of voices, the clink of glasses and cutlery — while separate microphones are picking up the speeches from very close range. This keeps the balance between the two entirely under your control in the post-production assembly of the programme, and means you don't have to cope with decisions on the day, when you may find that one of your speakers pitches their voice low enough for it to be overwhelmed by the camera microphone's recording of the background clatter of knives on plates.

The ideal arrangement would be a microphone — either a radio mike, or a conventional microphone on a long lead, well concealed from the camera — for each main speaker. One for the bride's father, one for the best man and one for the groom covers most eventualities, though you will need additional mikes for any extra speakers. The alternative is to have a microphone on the table which can be moved to each new speaker in turn, although it would probably be a good idea to brief someone to move it between speeches while you concentrate on shooting what is actually happening. If you follow this option, you will also have to be careful to make any adjustments to compensate for successive speakers being markedly louder or quieter than those who spoke before them, and to make the adjustments smoothly and quickly so that the whole soundtrack is consistently clear and well balanced.

If you're setting out to shoot the speeches in their entirety, you will be forced to keep the camcorder running throughout so that you don't miss any of the

A bird's-eye view of the reception, showing — a good compromise position for both the principals at the top table *and* some of the other guests at the smaller tables.

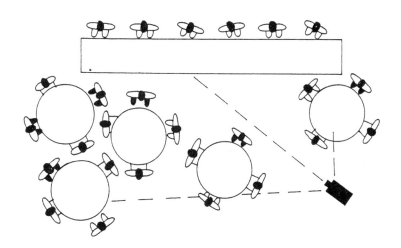

sound. Once again, this means checking batteries and tapes before you start, so you know you won't miss anything by having to stop to switch to a new tape or a new battery mid-speech — or in the all-too-brief gap between a toast and the speech which follows it. It also means keeping the picture varied, which we'll discuss in detail in a later chapter. At this stage, it's worth remembering that the more information you have on what each speech will contain, the more chance you have of suiting your pictures to what is actually being said. For example, if the best man's speech — which is almost bound to incorporate memories of growing up together which the groom would prefer to forget — also brings in other friends who will be present, then knowing roughly when this reference will be coming up enables you to pan across to pick up the friends' reactions to their being mentioned in the speech. But be aware of the dangers of people forgetting their lines, missing out particular sections of the script altogether, or covering them in the wrong order. Try to keep thinking on your feet, responding to what they actually say stage by stage. Only make a particular move, in camera terms, when you know beyond doubt that they're building up to a definite joke or reminiscence, and you're less likely to be caught out.

The cake and the cards

One of your subjects for a cutaway, or a sequence in its own right, on the wedding day will be the cake — and the most important part it plays in the proceedings is when the initial cut is made by the bride and groom, before the rest is whisked away to be cut into slices for distribution to the guests. One of your recce priorities will be to determine exactly where the cake will be placed, where the bride and groom will stand to cut it, which way they will face, and so on. After considering points like camera position, light levels and the problems which might be caused by any windows in the background, you need to find out whether this part of the reception is being covered by the official photographer. If it is, then once again you can leave directing the shoot on the day to him. He'll marshal the couple into the right position by the cake, organise repeats and retakes, close-ups and different angles, to suit his purposes. You can profit from this by shooting the subject he's arranging for you, not forgetting some footage of him delivering his own patter and directing his subjects, as part of your fly-on-the-wall view of everything that happens.

Another familiar and well-loved part of the reception routine is the reading out of the greetings cards and messages which have come in from the friends and relatives who, for various reasons, couldn't actually make it to the wedding. This can vary, however, in how and when it's done — which can be either as part of the best man's speech, following his toasting of the bridesmaids, or perhaps at a later moment in the routine altogether. Once again, if you're to shoot this part of the routine it's probably worth capturing in its entirety, as all the names and messages will mean a great deal to the couple and their families. Check how many cards there are likely to be. If there's a danger that there'll be a whole flood of cards, and that the messages they contain will overwhelm your coverage of the reception and distort the balance of the programme, then try and agree an order of priorities with your clients. Pick out the most important cards, the most unusual or the most interesting. If you can arrange for the best man to read this selection first, then you can limit your coverage to these and fade out pictures and sound before he goes on too long with all the others.

Drawing to a close

After these various landmarks in the proceedings, you should be close to planning the ending of your programme. This is another area where you have to respond to what is actually intended to happen. After the reception, it's usual for the bride and groom to go and change from their wedding outfits to clothes they will wear when they leave on their honeymoon, but there are variations which you need to discuss and take into account in your planning. Will the bride stop to throw her bouquet to her friends, according to the old tradition? Will they go straight from the table to change their clothes, or will they spend some time mingling with their families and their friends in the reception room first?

Either way you'll need to cover what's happening, while preparing for the closing sequence of the whole programme. If they're leaving on their honeymoon journey straight away, by car, by taxi to the airport, or whatever, then this gives you a natural conclusion to your programme. Alternatively, if they're simply disappearing for a while, only to reappear for the evening disco — perhaps departing on the honeymoon journey the following day — then you will have more of a problem with the ending.

One option might be to set up a departure (if your clients do not feel this would be too artificial), even if all that happens is that they drive round the block before returning to the hotel, eventually to reappear in the evening. If that's the case you may not have the use of a taxi, since one wouldn't have been booked, so you may have to use a car belonging to one of the family, or one of the guests. Another possibility is to shoot the preparation of the car in the traditional way: boots and tin cans being tied to the rear bumper, slogans and notices being sprayed on, or fastened to, the car, confetti being packed into every vacant space. Then all you need is the couple bidding their friends goodbye, emerging from the hotel entrance, rushing into the car and driving off amid cheers and waves from all concerned.

This doesn't have to be the final word on the ending, or indeed the very last picture sequence you and your audience will see on the screen. If the ending doesn't feel strong or graphic enough to round off the programme, you can fall back on one or two different techniques after the shoot is over. You can use special effects; building up a montage of shots from the preparations, the wedding and the reception over a suitable music track, using some of the official stills pictures, together with — for example — postcards from the honeymoon, overlaid with some closing message to suit your clients. We'll look at ideas like these in greater detail later in the book — for the time being we need to stop planning, and start shooting.

Shooting 1.
The Preparations

Providing all the pre-planning and recces, coupled with the detailed discussions with the couple most closely involved with the wedding, have been carried out thoroughly, you should feel able to approach the actual shoot with the confidence that you'll be able to do the event justice. Certainly, you're likely to have a busy day, but it's also likely to be an enjoyable one. There will be problems, no matter how careful and comprehensive the plans you've drawn up. But, with any luck, the amount of preparation you will have done will prevent these from seriously interfering with your successful coverage of a very important event.

We'll begin with the preparations, assuming, as suggested in Chapter Four, that you arranged to shoot some or all of these on the previous day. The simpler of the two preparation options is to begin with the groom and best man, and here you'll want to capture the final stages of the process — the buttoning up of the shirts, the knotting of the ties (or the arranging of the stocks or cravats if they're wearing formal morning coats). As you'll be cutting to and fro between this location and the home of the bride, and this section will be preceded by the opening sequence (either shots of the outside of the church, or the build-up of family photographs, as described earlier), you won't need an establishing shot in the conventional sense. Instead, it might be worth pulling out from, say, the best man's reflection in the mirror as he combs his hair, to reveal him and the groom rushing to finish their preparations.

If you are be shooting this sequence the day before the wedding, it's a good idea to let the action flow for a while, shooting the whole of the shirt-buttoning, tie-straightening, buttonhole-fixing, jacket-donning procedure as a single, fairly wide two-shot. You can then persuade them to go back to the beginning and repeat the whole process, as similar to the original in positions and movements as possible for continuity reasons. This time, go for the close-ups of faces, hands, and other details. If you can persuade them to inject a note of urgency, so much the better. A close-up of hands fumbling to do up shirt buttons, or to fasten cuff links, tells a story of haste, anxiety, tension and drama which does justice to the build-up we're trying to get across on tape, as we, and our audience, look forward to the ceremony.

Because you're trying to suggest haste in the sequence, try to keep your shots as brief as possible. If the best man is having trouble with his tie or his cuff links, cut away to something else when the shot has lasted two or three seconds, or the pace will slacken too much. If there's a clock on the wall, or even a watch on the dressing table or the sideboard, use this to show the passing of time, and to hint at urgency. (Since you're shooting this before the wedding day, you'll need to adjust the time to whatever would be right for the actual day.)

Because you are keeping your shots as brief as possible, many of them can be shot with a hand-held camera, which will also make it easier for you to move about if the rooms are small. But keep your eye open for the occasional longer shot to vary the picture and the pace, and provide additional visual interest. For example, a shot of the groom pinning on his buttonhole — while checking his reflection in the bathroom mirror — could be done as a zoom shot from the landing, or even looking up from the stairs if this is possible.

Sound, too, is important. You won't be using a commentary on the final programme, and there are limited areas where music can be effective on its own, so you need some dialogue between the people seen on screen. Ask them to imagine it's the day of the wedding, and time really *is* short, so they'll say the kind of things to one another which will sound convincing. How much longer is the groom going to be? The car will be outside any minute — doesn't he *want* to get married? Has the best man got the ring? Don't try anything elaborate or over-ambitious; the target is to add a bit of life to the pictures with snatches of believable conversation. Even another family member calling up from downstairs — asking how much longer they're going to be — is worth including. It all helps a set-up shoot look and sound convincing.

If you remember the pre-planning, you'll recall we need to end this sequence with the groom and best man leaving on their way to the church. This way we can make their departure clear to the audience in the final edited sequence, while they see the bride, her parents, and the bridesmaids, still finishing their preparations. Your recce will have told you how to end the bride's sequence with her and her father leaving for the church, so your overriding priority, in deciding how to finish the sequence of the groom and best man, is to find a different way of suggesting their departure. If you intend to shoot the bride and her father leaving the room and walking out to the hall and the front door, you could end the parallel sequence with a shot from an upstairs window, of the groom and the best man running out to their parked car, starting up, and accelerating off up the road *en route* to the church — one day early!

The bride's preparations

Now let's switch to covering the preparations at the bride's home. Since we want these to last longer, to emphasise the fact that the bride and her father will be arriving at the church after the arrival of the

Pre-wedding preparations: go for the candid and natural shots of people getting ready, bridging gaps with cutaways to show the passing of time.

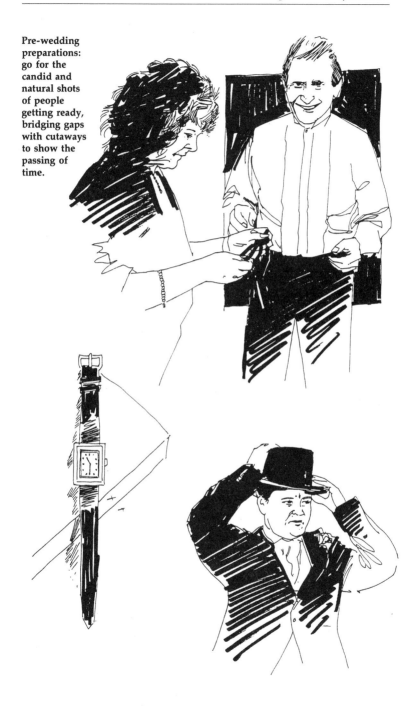

groom, best man and guests, we need to build up a longer and more detailed sequence. We should already have decided, in the planning stage, how much of the preparations to include in this sequence. For example, do we limit our shots to the bride herself getting ready? This would be difficult, as we need a ready source of cutaways to cover gaps in the action. Do we limit our coverage to the bride and her father? This is a better idea, as cross-cutting between two of the principal people in the story forms the basis of a brisk and entertaining sequence. Do we include the bride's mother? The bride is hardly likely to want to leave her out of the story, even during this brief, introductory section of the wedding video. Then there may be bridesmaids and pages staying at the bride's home and needing to get ready, and they could be included too.

However, you have one powerful ally on your side in trying to keep things simple and manageable. The plan was to shoot this the day before, so you can agree with the bride's family just how much should be included in the preparation sequence. If it's simply the bride and her parents, you have the basis of a varied introduction to the church and the ceremony which won't be too complicated to shoot, and which won't last too long when edited. *Because* it's the day before, there's no need to involve bridesmaids and relatives, pages and attendants, unless you and the family want them to be involved.

So far as shots and sequences are concerned, the same points we covered in the groom's preparation sequence apply here too. Keep shots brief, simple and varied. There are points where you'll have to compromise with reality. For example, is the bride planning to have her hair styled on the morning of the wedding day? If so, you'll have to watch out for possible continuity problems. Shots of any stages in the preparation which would happen before the styling was done present no problems — the bride being greeted by her mother with an early-morning cup of tea for example — but those shots where, on the day itself, the styling would have already been completed do need care. Try to avoid giving the game away by lingering on close-ups of the bride which show her unstyled hair in detail. One option would be to shoot the bride in the early stages of preparation, then concentrate more on the parents — with shots of the bride's father putting on his morning coat, adjusting his tie and combing his hair, and the bride's mother finishing her make-up and trying on her hat — before her father knocks on the door to ask if she's ready. This time you can cut from a shot of his face as he asks her the question, in close-up, to a medium shot, from just behind him, which reveals the bride ready in her wedding outfit. The result is the maximum impact with the minimum of emphasis on the details of her hair, especially if it's hidden under a hat or veil.

Of course, this will only be necessary if the styling is to be elaborate. With fashionably short and simple hairstyles the continuity may not present a problem and you can have complete freedom in what you choose to shoot. As before, the trick is to vary the shots within the overall objective of keeping them brief, simple and interesting. Also, monitor the rate at which you're using tape, as this should tell you whether you're shooting enough material or whether, as is more likely if this is your first wedding video, you're shooting far too much. Five minutes for the preparation sequences is a fairly sensible target which won't leave you too short of material, and won't mean too much work at the post-production stage to boil it down to a reasonable running time. Ten minutes can be lived with, but anything much more than that is definitely a case of overkill.

Looking for individuality

Many wedding videos will involve covering this kind of sequence in much the same way, so always be on the lookout for little human touches which help it to be individual to the couple involved. If the bride is preparing for her wedding in a room which has been hers since childhood, there will almost inevitably be reminders of her growing up, which you can use as cutaways or linking devices. A framed picture on the wall from a family holiday, or of her posing beside her first pony, gives you an ideal device for a zoom or a pan to her making the final adjustments to the wedding dress. The possibilities of shots like these will vary with the geometry of the room, but if you're shooting on the day before the wedding, you can afford to be a little more ambitious than you could on the day itself. You can move pictures about to give a camera angle and position which will produce the shot you're striving for. You could even use a different room, and 'dress' it as you'd dress a studio set with props (items from the genuine room). But first check with your subject that this is acceptable. One of the considerations which set wedding videos apart from most other programmes is that the subjects are the most important part of your audience, and it may be important to them that the rooms, and the settings, are those they know and find familiar.

Here, again, you need sound to back up your pictures and create the illusion of reality. A little time spent briefing your subjects beforehand will pay dividends; try to explain that you want them to think themselves as convincingly as possible into treating the setup as a genuine preparation for the wedding. If it seems natural to the bride to ask her parents how she looks, and for them to tell her she looks beautiful, this will work far more convincingly if it's a spontaneous question and reaction, than it will if you tell them what to say and when to say it.

In some ways the whole shoot may well work better if you brief your subjects on what you want, and then let it happen from start to finish — covering it as best you can, as you would the event itself. The difference is, in this case, that once you have the whole sequence safely on tape, you can play it back, and make a note of the gaps and omissions. Make a list of the shots you'd like to add to what you have — cutaways and close-ups, reaction shots and linking shots — and, as this is a setup for the camera's benefit, you have the supreme luxury of being able to go back and shoot them again, one by one, without worrying about losing time, or about delaying the departure for the church.

Once your departure sequences are safely shot, you're well prepared for the day of the wedding, and the different kind of shooting this will involve. From now on, the factors which will be under your control will be strictly limited, and your careful planning and recces will have to suffice to keep you ahead of the game. But the one or two well-covered preparation sequences will help you set the style for the entire programme, and reassure you that the production is safely under way.

CHAPTER 7

Shooting 2.
The Ceremony

From now on we have crossed the border between sequences specially set-up for the camera, to events which will happen in an order of their own, and at a pace of their own — whether you're in place and ready to record them or not. So your first priority must be a sound, well-thought-out and comprehensive plan, built up during the course of your recces, which takes care of all of the major decisions on the day. This should leave you free to devote your time almost entirely to the details of the shoot — to look out for your next subject, decide on the framing, start recording, decide when to cut and what the following subject should be. You're still going to be one of the busiest people present, but at least if you're well enough prepared you will have a fighting chance of being able to do the event justice.

The shoot begins with your arrival at the church, preferably well ahead of the groom and best man, and certainly ahead of the guests. This will give you the chance to shoot those exterior shots and cutaways which, assuming you didn't get to shoot them on your recce, or that you won't be banished to the outside of the church while the wedding ceremony is in progress, you won't be able to shoot at any other time during the day. Start with a long shot of the church, followed by some close-ups of details like the nameboard and noticeboard facing the road, the gate giving access from the roadside, the tower or spire, the windows, the porch, any carvings or gargoyles, any picturesque shrubs or stonework, close-ups of flowers, or even memorials. All of these shots can prove invaluable later in bridging gaps, avoiding difficult cuts, and providing links to suggest the passing of time later in the shoot.

Three detail shots to bridge the gap if you have to remain outside for the actual ceremony.

If time allows, and the wedding you are covering isn't too closely following an earlier wedding, christening, or whatever, in the same church, you can now make contact with the minister to set up that part of your equipment which won't be needed until your shoot in the church begins. This will include your micro-

109

A simple tripod — with adjustable legs and a handle for controlling the camera position — and a set of 'baby-legs' for ground-level shots.

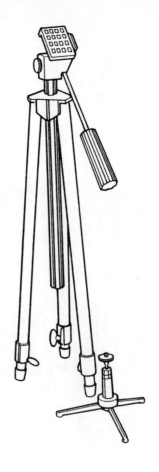

phones and cables, any background lights you decided would be needed from your recce of the church interior, any separate audio recorders to pick up the sounds of the ceremony, the tripod you may need if you are shooting from the back of the church — assuming you don't need it outside — and so on. This is where the preparation you did earlier will prove invaluable — you'll know where to put the mikes and the lights, where the cables should be run, where to plug into power sockets, where to set up the tripod, and all the other information which enables you to prepare quickly and efficiently.

Once the equipment inside the church has been set up, you're free to move back outside and carry on with the shoot. When the groom and best man arrive, you can decide whether you want to record them getting out of the car and walking up the path to the church, or whether — given the preparation sequences you shot the day before — you can cut straight to a shot of them talking quietly as they wait outside the church porch before going in. If they go in, you can then concentrate on the arrival of the guests who should soon be following them. Generally speaking, they'll all be walking down the same path in groups of twos, threes or more, so you'll have to work quickly to vary your shots. Work from both sides of the path, move close to the gate and back towards the porch, and shoot some shots as reverses, following groups towards the porch and into the church. Always look for moments of spontaneity; old friends greeting one another, children tugging at parents, and the subdued delight and anticipation on everyone's face of the happy event which brings them all together.

Shooting inside the church

As the guests continue to flock into the church, you have to decide at what point you wind up the shoot outside and move to *your* place inside the church. This depends on a number of factors, including the timetable which is now developing. How many of the guests have you been able to cover so far, and how imminent is the arrival of the bride? Another pointer to your decision is the position you will be taking up inside the church to record the ceremony. If you will be shooting from beside the couple at the front of the church as the ceremony proceeds, you won't be able to cover the bride and her father walking up and entering the church. You'll have to be in position inside the church before that, so that the first your camera sees of the bride and her father will be when they make their entrance and start the walk down the aisle towards the altar.

111

If, on the other hand, your position is limited to the back of the church, then one advantage is that you can shoot a close-up sequence of the bride preparing to make her entrance — always a moment of spontaneous drama. You can wait outside, until the last possible moment, for a shot of the bride and her father pausing outside the church and then walking towards the door. If you have been able to agree with them to pause for a few seconds at this point, you can move ahead of them into your position at the back of the church, and then start shooting again as they appear in the porch and turn to start their walk down the aisle. As they move away from you, you can follow them as far as possible with your zoom. But this will require some care since your focus will have to change as the distance between you and your subjects increases. If time allows, this is something you could practise with the last of the guests, or by asking one of the ushers to walk slowly from the porch to the front of the church and back. (You could also have practised this at the rehearsal if time allowed.) Your depth of field will be restricted in the subdued light inside the church, and the time to practise your focus adjustment is before the irreplaceable shot of bride and father on their way to join the groom and best man at the front of the church.

Once everyone is inside the church, and the ceremony begins, you will need to keep several points in mind. Is there a musical accompaniment to the wedding, from the church organ or a choir? If so, you may need a track of this in full, to simplify your editing later on — otherwise you will only pick up snatches of the music with each shot, which could cause severe continuity problems. You also need to change batteries and tapes before starting to record the ceremony, in order to have the maximum recording time at your disposal. From your pre-planning you have an order of priorities for what to record during the wedding service, and also some idea of which sections will need cutting or simplifying, and how and where to make the cuts. If, for example, the minister is going through the familiar preamble to the service with the words laid down in the prayer book, you might decide that, once the reading is firmly established for the audience, you can safely allow a gap in your coverage.

Assuming that, at this point, you're shooting with the camcorder mounted on its tripod, all you need to do is fade sound and vision by using the fade-out facility. Take care not to move the camcorder while your recording is being interrupted, and then, when you're ready to come back in again, pick the tail end of the minister's speech (which you should be able to check from the prayer book and the order of service) and use the fade-in facility on the camcorder. Because the tripod will have kept the framing constant, you can use this fast fade-out, fade-in technique to bridge deliberate gaps easily and unobtrusively, while still making it clear that time is passing.

When you reach the responses, it's essential to capture them in their entirety and, although at this point the service is not under your control as director, you do have the next best thing — a script, in that the precise details of the minister's instructions, and the bride's and groom's responses, are laid down in a definite order. This allows you to make the most of this section of the service from a creative point of view. As the minister gives his introduction, you can shoot him with the couple as a three-shot, closing in on the groom as he begins to repeat his responses, moving to the bride when it's her turn, and moving out to a two-shot of the couple when the minister finally pronounces them husband and wife.

If you have to shoot from the back of the church your options are much more restricted. Apart from slow zooms in and out to show the couple and the minister in close-up and in long shot, you're limited to the occasional cutaways of whichever of the guests you can shoot across the church, necessary to avoid a succession of anonymous backs. Here you'll find the layout of more modern churches, which are often based on a squarer ground plan than the long, narrow nave of traditional churches, helps provide you with a more varied range of subjects to use as the service proceeds.

In other respects you have the same priorities in terms of what you capture. Whenever you want a pause in the coverage, all you have to do is pull back to a long shot of the couple, seen over the heads of the guests, and fade to black. Fade the picture and sound back up again when you want to resume shooting and, when you know the responses are imminent, you can begin a slow zoom up the aisle towards the couple and the minister. Since this time you are focused on the far end of the zoom throughout, there

Shooting at the front of the church allows you a three-shot of the couple and minister, a two-shot of the couple and close-ups of each individual.

Shooting from the back of the church: your shots will be improved it you can shoot from a gallery for an elevated viewpoint, and if you can persuade the couple to face one another when exchanging their vows.

will be no need to change focus over the course of the zoom — provided you checked that the group at the front of the church was in sharp focus *before* you pulled back to begin the zoom in.

115

Timing is the key here. Ideally, you want to be reaching the end of the zoom just as the groom starts to make his responses, guided by the minister. With a little luck, or a spot of pre-arrangement, the groom will turn to his left to look at his bride while he makes the responses. This at least gives you a chance for a profile shot of him speaking, rather than a back view. In fact, if the bride looks at him while he's speaking, and vice versa, and they stand so that the minister is framed in between them, you have a very effective three-shot at the end of the zoom, provided the power of your lens and the length of the church don't place it too far off to be captured.

Signing the register

Once the ceremony is finished, you have the option of shooting the signing of the register or waiting for the bride and groom to emerge, walk down the aisle, and appear outside for the taking of the photographs. The decision will depend above all on the wishes of the couple, and on whether the minister gives his permission. If you *are* needed to cover the signing of the register, you need to have sized up the location in your recce. Will you have a clear view? Is it light enough, or will you need extra lighting? These contingencies will have to be checked and provided for so that, on the day, you have time to deal with the lighting — and get yourself into position without delaying the proceedings too much. With a church full of guests waiting for the couple to reappear and the photography to begin, not to mention a minister who may have another wedding due in half an hour, you'll be under some pressure to deliver the results in as little time as possible.

Depending on the configuration of the room in which you're shooting, you will have to cover the action as best you can. The ideal would be a camera position which allowed you to face the couple across the desk or table where the register is placed for signing or, failing that, to look from one end, with the couple on one side of your frame and the minister on the other. To save time, you will probably have to cover the whole procedure in a single shot, closing in slowly from a three-shot to cover the action of the husband signing the register, ending on his hand as he performs the actual signature. Cut back to the face of his wife watching, pull back to a three-shot to see the pen being handed to her, and then close in again for her signature. Finally, pull back out for the shot of the husband's face as he watches, and then pull back again for a closing three-shot as the minister congratulates them and they head out of the room, back to the body of the church. You might be able to follow a similar strategy for the signing of the register by the two witnesses.

This long, continuous shot will capture all the sound effects and snatches of conversation between the three, while still allowing you to cut it into different single shots when you come to edit the sequence together in post-production. You can then either cut straight to the scene outside the church where the photographs are being taken — or you could persuade the minister and the couple to wait a moment or two while you move back into the church to record their walk down the aisle, or move outside

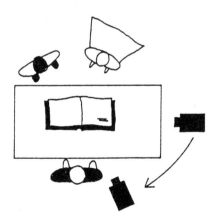

An aerial view of the signing of the register, showing how you can cover all three individuals from one corner of the room, or the couple from across the desk.

and wait for them to emerge for the taking of the photographs. This way you will end up with the best of both worlds.

Shooting from outside the church

What happens if you aren't allowed to shoot in the church at all? As we said in an earlier chapter, the next best option is the chance to record the sound at least. Assuming that you have someone else able to look after the recording of the sound within the church, this leaves you to shoot some cutaways which can be used over the soundtrack — particularly the responses — of the ceremony afterwards. Part of this will involve the cutaways around the church that you shot earlier, though there may be one or two extra possibilities now that the wedding is actually in progress. The cars waiting outside, the clock showing the time of the wedding, any onlookers waiting by the gate for the couple to emerge — all are useful options. But they can't cover the gap on their own. If you fade down the soundtrack, so it sounds like the minister's words filtering out to the churchyard outside, that will cover part of the ceremony. But once you reach the point where the couple are about to speak their responses, you need a more specific shot to relate to

If you aren't allowed to shoot inside the church at all, you may have to shoot the bride and her father entering the church from outside . . .

. . . tilt up to the tower (top left), close in to the clock (bottom left), then fade out the clock (bottom right), and fade back in again as the service finishes (top right) ready to . . .

. . . tilt down to the church doorway in time to shoot the couple emerging as husband and wife at the end of the ceremony.

the words. You could use some of the official photographer's stills, re-shot and edited together during post-production, or you can keep your eyes open for possibilities arising during the official photography session, which we'll come to next.

First, however, we'll consider the problem of how to cope with a blanket refusal to allow *any* recording — audio or video — inside the church. Faced with this kind of limitation, all you can do is cover the entry of the groom, the best man and the guests into the church, followed by the arrival of the bride and her father. You'll then need a device to allow you to emphasise the passing of time — to show that the ceremony has taken place without your being able to cover it — so that when your next shot shows the couple emerging for the photographs to be taken, it's clear to the audience that the marriage ceremony has been completed.

One ideal option is our old friend the church clock. Set up your camera in position on the tripod, so you can tilt upwards from your closing shot of the bride and her father entering the church to find and frame up the clock. Pause a couple of seconds for both the shot and the time displayed to register, then activate the fade-out facility and leave the camera in position while you take a break.

All you need now is for someone to help you from inside the church by giving you an agreed signal when the bride and groom are returning down the aisle after signing the register. If you get your timing right —and it will need a little bit of practice, preferably during the recce, to determine exactly how long it will take them to walk the length of the aisle and emerge through the church doorway — you can activate the fade-up facility to bring up the picture of the clock showing the new time, and then tilt down just as the bride and groom emerge from the doorway for the official photography session.

What can you do if the church in question doesn't have a clock? The answer is to look for something else which shows the passing of time; on a sunny day you might be able to use the movement of a shadow thrown by a shrub or tree against the wall of the church, or across the path. Another, more foolproof method of showing time passing is available to those who have one of the more sophisticated types of camcorder, with a time-lapse or animation facility. If this is the case, all you have to do is set up to look at the church in a long shot, with the camcorder itself firmly fixed on the tripod. Then you shoot a series of very brief glimpses of the same scene, rather as a time-lapse sequence would be built up, using the animation facility in the recorder to assemble-edit the sequence together.

Because there will inevitably be changes taking place in the frame — the clouds will move across the sky, people may wander in and out of shot, shadows will shift and patches of sun and shade will come and go — the speeding up of these changes by means of the time-lapse effect will serve to emphasise the passing of time very clearly indeed. All you need is a short sequence of around five to ten seconds, before you can safely pause to wait for the signal from inside the church that the couple are on their way, and you can start zooming in to pick them up as they emerge from the porch.

If you can't find a way of showing the passing of time in the picture, then the best way to cope is to return to the fade-out, fade-in technique on the church door, but make the fade take a little longer before coming back into the picture. This does at least enable you to avoid the danger of mistiming the tilt down from the church clock, or the pan from the shadows. By emphasising the fade out and fade in rather more obviously, the message about the passing of time will reach your audience, especially when set against the familiar surroundings of a wedding.

The photography session

Now let's move on to the taking of the photographs. As we mentioned in an earlier chapter, it's advisable to let the official photographer do the directing for you, since he or she forms part of the scene which you're intent on capturing. Because the pictures will undoubtedly start with the just-married couple, begin with a shot of them as they emerge from the church — happy the ceremony is safely over and enjoying being the centre of attention, or shyly putting up with the spotlight being turned on them for a few more minutes.

After a close two-shot of the couple readjusting to being back outside, and starting to respond to the photographer's instructions, pull back in a zoom —or start a new shot with a wider framing — to show the photographer in shot as well, so that the context will be quite clear. Another option, if by now you've taken the camera off the tripod, is to move to one side of the couple (but not close enough so you will be in the photographer's way) and shoot a brief shot of the photographer squinting through the viewfinder and looking up to marshal the couple into the right place for the picture. Then move back to the couple, and try to record them at the instant that your camera microphone picks up the click of the shutter taking the official picture.

From this point onwards you should be conscious of the need to vary the material as much as possible, while still covering all the principal members of both families. If this wasn't enough to think about on its own, you also need to be aware of how much material you're shooting — this is an important interlude in the main business of the day, but, after all, still an interlude. And finally, you need to be aware of the passing of time yourself. If you decided, as discussed earlier, that you don't need to capture the bride and groom leaving on the way to the reception, then you *do* need to leave ahead of them, so you can be ready to shoot as soon as they arrive.

Try to alternate your subjects between the formal groupings assembled by the official photographer, and the jokes and chatter between different members of the families as they shuffle into line, the onlookers waiting for their turn to join the group, and those guests who have followed the families out of the church to watch the pictures being taken, before they make their own way to the reception. Don't forget the occasional long shot of the scene, and the cutaways of the photographer at work. If your shots of the photographer are recorded as reverses (with your back to the group that's being assembled for the official pictures and your framing tight on the camera and its operator), then these will be invaluable for editing. There shouldn't be any continuity problems caused by the stage of the photography session at which they were actually recorded.

This is another area where pre-planning can help give you advance warning of the need to move on to cope with other priorities. If you ask the photographer what shots have been requested, and the order in which he's planned to shoot them, then the groups you see being assembled will give you a close check on the progress being made. (You might have had the opportunity to discuss this before the wedding day.) Depending on the amount of coverage you were able to do inside the church — sound recording only, or video and sound recording from the front or back of the nave — you need to pack away the equipment you used, and which you won't need again until the reception. This will almost certainly mean microphones and cables, and it may include background lighting. Another wedding may be scheduled for later that same day at the church, and you need to pack your kit away with the minimum of delay and disruption.

Here too an assistant would be very helpful; if someone else can collect the equipment and transport it to your car while you concentrate on covering the shooting outside, that's another time-consuming chore safely taken care of. If your plan includes a shot of the bride and groom driving off into the distance on their way to the reception, you can safely leave the photographic session while the last shots are being taken, and set up your closing shot of this part of the programme with some care.

You will have picked the ideal spot on your recce, but you may need to rethink it slightly if people are in the way, or if the car isn't able to stop at exactly the spot you had in mind. If you can turn the camera back towards the photo session, and pick up the couple on their way out of the throng and heading for the car, you can make it into a nice long shot to round off the church-and-ceremony section with a flourish. But if the shot looks like lasting too long, while the couple's friends get in the way with clouds of confetti, have a cutaway in mind which will allow you to interrupt the continuum. Then you can use the start of the shot with them walking towards you, cut to the cutaway — perhaps someone getting ready to throw confetti — and cut back to them at the tail end of the shot climbing into the car and driving off to the reception. If you shoot the cutaway in any case — better still a selection of cutaways — you keep all your options open for when you edit the programme together in post-production.

Bad-weather options

So far we've made one overriding assumption which governs the kind of shooting we plan to do: we have assumed that the weather may be warm or cold, sunny or dull, windy or still, but that it will be dry. What do we do if the wedding happens to take place in a downpour? Much will depend on the nature of the rain, and how long it lasts. Occasional sharp showers, interspersed with spells of sunshine, pose a different kind of problem to steady drizzle, which is different again from a prolonged, soaking rainstorm.

Asides from looking out of the window on the morning of the wedding, or listening to a weather forecast the evening before, there isn't a great deal you can do in the way of recceing and pre-planning the weather factor in your shooting. You should ask the couple, during your initial discussions, what difference bad weather would make to the organisation of the day's events, since it's almost certain they must have considered the problem too. Some decisions are easy to predict: drinks on the lawn of the hotel before the reception proper would have to be moved inside, so in that sense the weather may affect the location but not the actual shoot. More to the point is how you plan to cope with those sections of the day which *have* to take place outside, like the move from car to church, and vice versa, and the taking of the official photographs (although in bad weather these may be delayed until the wedding party reaches the reception venue).

Let's look at the worst case first — the kind of prolonged, steady downpour which puts a blight on the most carefully planned day. All you can do is concentrate even more carefully on the interior sequences, which are, after all, the main areas of interest in the wedding. So far as the rain outside is concerned, it's part of the day's memories, so try to find some shots which show just how bad things were. For example, instead of shooting the bride and her father walking up the path to the church, you may be able to set up your camera inside the porch and shoot them running up the waterlogged path with umbrellas held over their heads to try and protect their outfits from the weather.

You could do likewise with the guests, although, as one soaked couple running through the rain looks very much like another, your material will be limited. Perhaps it would be better to cut your losses and try to capture more shots of the guests, as individuals, when they are safely dry and indoors at the reception. The photographic session too will pose problems, though at least the problems will be shared between you and the official photographer, so that you can respond to whatever contingency he introduces to cope with the situation. It's possible he might shoot the photographs with umbrellas held over those taking part to keep them dry. It's possible he might be able to find a sheltered spot, wholly or partly under cover, for the groups at least — though you yourself might have to shoot from outside. It's even a possibility that the photo session will be moved to the reception and the pictures taken indoors, in which case the problem has been solved for you.

If you *do* find you have to shoot some shots in the rain, be prepared to protect your camera and, if possible, yourself. Some manufacturers make fitted rain covers for their camcorders — in which case keeping one in the equipment bag is a good idea. Another alternative, if you have a helper on hand, is a really large golfing umbrella which can keep the rain off you and the camera while not intruding into the shot. But if the weather combines a strong and gusty wind with the rain, this may not be the most stable and reliable protection, so you may still have to fall back on a waterproof cover for your camera and a coat for yourself.

Showery weather offers a different kind of problem. Assuming conditions alternate between sunshine and rain, you can capture some quite pleasing effects provided you and your camcorder are properly pro- tected from the damp. A sudden rush for coats and umbrellas in the middle of the photographic session, for example, certainly provides plenty of spontaneity in an otherwise rather formal section of the pro- ceedings. However you may find that the constantly

Wet-weather expedients: make the weather work for you — by using shots of people running through the rain or sheltering from the downpour — providing you and your camcorder are properly protected.

changing lighting conditions make continuity difficult. To take the photo session as our example, imagine you have just recorded the couple preparing to pose

127

for their first formal picture, in bright sunshine. You move closer to them and then turn round to shoot a reverse shot of the cameraman getting ready to take his shot. If the sun vanishes behind a cloud when you do this, the resulting shot may look as if you took it at an entirely different time. And if the sun re-emerges by the time you move back to your original position for your next shot of the couple, that impression will be reinforced.

All this means you have two options: either you keep an eye on the weather, so you know when sunlight is going to disappear or when conditions are suddenly about to brighten up, or you insure against both contingencies. The chances are you will be watching the weather in any case, so you have the maximum warning of the next shower building up overhead. But when the timetable isn't in your hands, you often can't hurry your shots, or slow them down, in an effort to keep your conditions constant. Better, in that case, to go ahead and shoot your principal shots regardless. If you end up with a series of group photographs, some in sunshine and some in shadow, some even with umbrellas and rain in the picture, then concentrate on getting cutaways and reverses of the photographer at work, and of the other guests watching, in all these different conditions. Only if you're well covered for all the changes in the weather during the photographic session can you be sure that editing the sequence together afterwards will be a simple and straightforward process.

Happily, the next section of the programme is less dependent on the weather — the reception is usually planned so that the whole event can take place indoors if the weather changes for the worst. You may lose your planned sequence in the garden before the meal is served, but at least you will be able to shoot the guests having drinks and talking indoors instead. In fact the rest of the programme could be recorded indoors if the weather should make this necessary.

Shooting 3.
The Reception

Your first task, in shooting the wedding reception, is to get there as quickly as possible — certainly ahead of the guests and possibly ahead of the bridal couple, depending on the priorities you agreed with them at the planning stage of the programme. If you've managed to record the couple leaving the church, and you know that the guests will be welcomed with a drink on arrival at the reception, or be greeted by a receiving line, then you still need to move quickly; the setting up of the receiving line itself gives you a prime opportunity for an informal, behind-the-scenes introduction to another formal part of the event. If, on the other hand, you weren't committed to shooting the bride and groom leaving the church, then it would be sensible to pull out of the photography session early enough to leave time to reach the reception venue in comfort.

Your first priority, on arrival, depends on the results of your recce. Did you find that any of the different parts of the location required extra background lighting? If so, now is the moment to set it up according to the notes you took at the time. In most cases though, the combination of the performance of modern camcorders in low light levels, and the generally bright interiors of hotels and restaurants, should solve this problem for you. If this is the case you can start to sort out the microphones. We know from the earlier discussion on your priorities at the reception that you'll need a careful selection of different microphones to record all the speeches and toasts clearly and fully, in addition to picking up the background atmosphere sound on the camera mike. But will you need one or more of these microphones while you shoot the guests being greeted by the receiving line?

If you're shooting a receiving line, try shooting the people moving into position as a relaxed introduction to a more formal sequence.

Two points are worth bearing in mind here. When you're shooting the guests going through the receiving line, you will be much closer to the action than your position in the reception room will allow. You're also not so dedicated to recording high-quality sound; what's really needed is the buzz of conversation and the odd few words of greeting heard above the background chatter. This should easily be possible to secure on the camera microphone. If you do need a back-up microphone, a single mike on its own lead could be placed at the far end of the receiving line from your preferred camera position, to give you another source for your soundtrack. If this micro-phone picks up snatches of conversation which aren't synchronised with the picture you're recording at the time, the fact that your establishing shot will have shown a whole line of people all deep in conversation, and that many other conversations can be partly heard anyway, will prevent this from seeming odd, or looking like the result of an editing error.

When you're ready to start recording, begin with some shots of the receiving line assembling — capturing the various members of the family sorting themselves out into the right order will provide some relaxed moments, after which you can start framing up for the entrance of the first guests. As you will probably begin by setting up at the end of the line opposite the entrance, the first guests to appear will be at the far end of the line. Try picking them up in long shot and zooming in to frame them and the people they're speaking to in close-up at the end of the zoom, after focusing on the end of the receiving line *before* zooming out, so you know the shot will stay in focus.

After this, it's a question of covering the action in as varied and original a way as you can. Remember the advice given earlier, to keep your shots short and simple. In covering the receiving line sequence, it's probably better to discard the tripod after the first zoom-in shot, and then move round your subjects, shooting with a hand-held camcorder. Take some three-shots and four-shots — where couples are speaking to one or two members of the receiving line. Go for close-ups of individuals, some of them deep in conversation, some of them about to greet someone who's currently talking to the next person in line. Get some close-ups of people shaking hands as cutaways now and again, and move to the other side of the receiving line for reverse shots — so that some of your shots are facing the receiving line and others are facing the guests — and remember to look back along the line to include the occasional shot of guests moving away to enter the room where the reception is to be held.

How much should you shoot? This depends on three factors: how many people there are on the guest list, how many your couple positively want included in the programme (not necessarily the same number), and how many you have been able to capture earlier. Within these limits, it shouldn't really be necessary to shoot everyone being greeted by the receiving line, particularly if it's a large wedding. On the other hand, in the interests of balance, you need to be careful not to limit your coverage to the same people you may already have shot arriving at church, or watching the photo session in progress outside.

Once you feel that objective has been achieved, end on a shot of more of the guests leaving the end of the receiving line, on their way to the reception. To be doubly safe, shoot them walking away, from the viewpoint of other guests still passing down through the receiving line, then walk past the line and shoot a different group of guests walking towards the camera and out of frame on their way to the reception. This gives you two alternative end shots, so you can then move on to the reception room while guests are still arriving.

Simple alternative links

What happens if you don't have a formal setup — like a receiving line — with which to begin your coverage of the reception? If guests arrive in casual groups and drift into the reception, it may well be difficult for you to establish a structure to this new section of your programme as quickly as you would like. If this is the case, it might be simpler to choose a less ambitious link, as revealed in your initial reconnaissance. For example, we suggested earlier that the passing of time and change of place could be suggested by fading out a scene on the church clock before you leave for the reception, and then fading up again on a clock in the hotel, preferably located in the room where the reception is being held.

Of course there may not be a clock at the church and, even if there is, the clocks at the hotel may be in completely the wrong place for you to make any use of them. You may even have had to fall back on the clock at the church to show the passing of time during the ceremony (if you were forbidden to record inside the church). But that's no reason to avoid returning to the idea now for a second passing of time. In fact your audience will be more likely to recognise the device and to see it as a definite characteristic of the pro-gramme — and you could even use it again if you needed to. One further use of this link might be a shift from the afternoon reception to the start of the evening party, if the couple wanted the last shot of the programme to show them having the first dance together.

So don't be deterred if your recce didn't reveal any convenient clock faces in the reception room. We described earlier some of the ways of solving this problem; by having a clock moved into the room as part of the furniture, or using a small carriage clock among the wedding presents, if these are on show at the reception. We also looked at the possibility of setting up a deliberate link in another part of the hotel, possibly with a member of the hotel staff looking up at a clock or down at a wrist-watch, before walking through into the reception room followed by the camera. Your recce should have told you whether any of these options would be possible on the day — and whatever you eventually decided, now's the moment to put it into practice.

What do you do if you can't find such a convenient link, though? Look for something else is the answer; perhaps the flowers outside the church and a bunch of flowers as table decoration inside the reception (again as we described earlier in the planning and reconnaissance section). Or you could fade out on a shot of the bride and groom posing for a formal picture outside the church, and fade up on the miniature figures of the bride and groom often used as a decoration on the wedding cake, if this is placed in the reception room when the guests begin to arrive. Another possibility we mentioned earlier is a cut from a particular guest (preferably an individual who's easily identifiable, whether in indoor or outdoor clothing) shot at the church, to the same guest talking to friends and enjoying a drink at the reception. (If you plan to use this option, see if there is a particular guest the couple would like you to focus on.)

The common point with all of these different options is that they need to have been thought of, and evaluated, during the recce. Otherwise there is the danger that you may spot the perfect linking subject at the reception, but lack the right shot at the church to make the link in the programme. It's also important to remember that, while a link is desirable on the grounds of economy and style, it isn't absolutely essential. If you do lack a subject which suggests a cut between two appropriate shots at the two different locations, then don't be too disappointed. If there isn't a receiving line to give you a properly planned start to the reception, then don't worry too much either. What's needed, instead, is a strong opening shot which says 'reception' to the audience in no uncertain terms.

Buffet and table-service receptions

The actual subject you choose depends on the way the reception has been planned. Let's assume, for argument's sake, that it takes the form of a buffet, where guests queue up for helpings from dishes laid out on a long table, before going to sit down at other tables where they will proceed to enjoy the meal, listen to the speeches and drink the toasts as the reception progresses. In this case your opening shot could be framed up, using the tripod for extra steadiness, on one of the waiters or waitresses cutting slices from a joint of meat and putting them on a guest's plate —or a shot of one of the guests dipping a serving spoon into a bowl of salad. Once the subject has been established in close-up, you can then pull out to reveal the laden table and the line of guests, and the location and the occasion will be clear to your audience at once.

There are other possibilities for unusual shots, especially if the food being served at the buffet is varied and colourful. Go for as many close-ups as possible of the different dishes, and of food being passed over and piled onto the plates. Go for close-ups of the faces too: of guests concentrating on the serving of food, waiting for their turn, or talking to their neighbours in the queue. If the buffet is being served from a square or rectangular table with queues on both sides, you can shoot reverse shots without moving your camera position, once there are no problems over continuity to give away the fact you're only shooting from one side of the table. If the table is a long one with a queue down one side, try shooting from the end down along the table. Here, particularly if you lower your camcorder position to just above table level, you can pick out some good rhythmic shots of the line of faces, and a bewildering forest of hands, spoons and forks ladling portions of different dishes from the buffet onto the plates. Because your depth of field will be restricted when shooting indoors, you may even be able to produce some unusual change-focus shots. Because the buffet is likely to be in progress for some time, and because you will know when it's coming to an end by monitoring the length of the queue, you can afford to experiment with some unusual and ambitious shots without missing important subjects or shooting opportunities elsewhere in the room.

A bird's-eye view of a buffet, and the two camera positions which will allow you to capture most of the action.

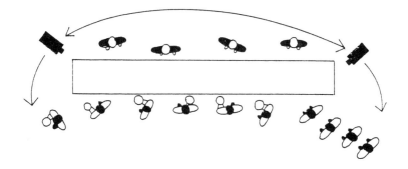

135

So far as ending the serving sequence is concerned, pull back to some wider shots of people leaving the queue, and pan across the room to show them taking their seats. This kind of shot has the advantage that it's also establishing the location as a whole for the next section of the reception — the speeches and the toasts which will follow in the programme. Once everyone has taken their seats and started to eat, your coverage can be fairly brief — all we need to establish is that the meal is in progress, with a few shots of diners eating and conversing with their neighbours. Vary your subjects between guests, in general, and the bride, groom and their families in particular. But don't let this part of the sequence go on too long.

How can you begin your reception coverage when instead of a stand-up buffet the meal is served to the guests sitting at their tables by a team of waiters and waitresses? In this case our initial requirement is the same. We need a graphic image which says 'reception', in close-up, from which we can move quickly to set that close-up image in its wider context. This needs a little bit more thought than was the case with the buffet, but the principle is the same.

Try setting up your camcorder when the first course is about to be served. This time you'll need a tripod, and you need to zoom in close to show the table in front of the bride where the first plate will be placed when the waiters and waitresses come in. Once you've focused sharply and you're ready to release the button and start recording, watch for the entrance of the serving team with the first-course portions. As soon as they come into the room, start shooting with a fade-up from black — by keeping one eye on the subject through the viewfinder and leaving your other eye open, you can time your shot so that the fade-up ends just before the plate is placed in front of the bride. Pause a second to let the shot establish itself in the minds of the audience, then zoom back slowly to show the table, the waiters and waitresses, and the start of the meal. You can reinforce this opening shot with a succession of shots of plates being placed in front of guests in other parts of the room. Then you can concentrate on building up a short, but varied, sequence of the meal being enjoyed — exactly as described for the buffet-based reception — and end on a fade to black when you have enough material.

Preparing for the speeches

Before you can shoot the speeches and the toasts which form the most important part of the reception, you need to have microphones in place. One option is to place these in position before the reception begins, and there's no reason why this should not be your approach — except that you may be fully occupied shooting the introductory sequence and, if you're using cable rather than radio mikes, there's always the danger that people walking to and fro across the room may trip up or knock your microphones out of position. On the other hand, with the meal safely in progress, no one's going to worry if you take a few minutes to set up your microphones and arrange the cables as planned in your recce of the reception room. Then you need to take advantage of this pause in the proceedings — apart from taking the opportunity to have something to eat and drink yourself — to check your tapes and batteries. The section we're about to record, with speeches and toasts, is another one where it's imperative you don't leave any gaps because of the batteries or the tapes running out.

Assuming all is ready for the longest and most important section of your coverage of the reception, you can relax and enjoy the meal. But be on the watch for the serving of the last course. Once the diners, particularly those on the top table, start eating this, then it's time to be back on duty. You need to be able to rely on a signal from the best man, as agreed by prior arrangement, to warn you when he's about to attract the attention of the assembled guests. It would be best, if you can, to arrange for him to give you an agreed sign two minutes before he calls the room to attention, so you can set your camcorder running, adjust the tripod (from now on a tripod is almost essential in order to avoid fatigue when recording the speeches in full), frame up the opening picture, and start recording by fading up from black as he starts to say his piece.

What should this opening shot be? Cast your mind back to the previous sequence which showed the diners enjoying their meal. Our first need is for a shot which manages to show the meal is now over, as well as introduce the speeches-and-toasts section of the reception. If you know that the best man is going to try to attract everyone's attention by tapping a knife against his wine glass, you might be able to frame up a shot showing an empty plate left from the meal, a glass, and his hand picking up the knife to make the signal. If there's a danger that all the plates will be cleared away by this time, ask the waiters to leave one in shot as a use of creative licence. Then all you have to do is fade up on the plate and glass as the best man starts to call for everyone's attention, and pull out to show him in wide shot as he begins to speak to the guests.

From now on you will have a set of different events to record. It may be that the bride and groom are asked to cut the cake at this point and, if your plan shows this is next, you need to have worked out how to record it. In most cases, it takes an appreciable time for the couple to pose for pictures, to set the knife in position and actually make the cut, and if this is another moment when the official photographer is involved, you can rely on him or her to do your directing for you. All you have to remember is to vary your shots and your viewpoint as much as possible. If you were prudent enough to secure some really tight close-ups of the decoration of the cake when you first arrived, these can prove very useful as cutaways when editing the cake-cutting part of the ritual down to a manageable length.

Shooting the speeches

The more you know about what each person intends to say and the order in which they mean to say it, together with a rough running-time for the speeches, the better prepared you'll be to do them justice in visual terms, as well as in terms of the sound you record. As explained earlier, the only way to capture all the speeches on audio is to leave the camera running throughout — and the only way to avoid boring pictures is to keep moving from subject to subject, and to relate the subject of the picture to what's being said whenever possible.

So the ideal brief is a full script of what each speech will contain. You may have to work with much less than that, however, as many of the people delivering the speeches may be doing so with less than a complete transcript of what they're planning to say. In fact, those who are more experienced and more confident at delivering speeches may be relying on a set of outline notes, or even a series of key headings on a piece of paper, to aid their memory. But the chances are they will deliver the speech profes-sionally, covering all their points in the right order and keeping closely to the target time. It's the more nervous and less experienced speakers you need to be wary of; whether they have a series of notes scribbled on the back of an envelope, or a word-perfect script, the chances are that they may lose their way, tell their stories in the wrong order, or even miss some out altogether. They may ramble on too long, or finish with a sudden switch to proposing their toast, almost before you realise it. It's your job to capture all this, in its entirety, as creatively as you can. And you need to be constantly on your guard for unexpected changes throughout this part of the proceedings.

Let's assume that your first speaker is about to rise to his feet in response to the best man's announcement. Start with a fairly wide shot of the principal table, showing both the best man and the speaker, as the introduction is delivered. As the speaker begins his delivery, close in on him fairly slowly, and hold him in close-up for around ten to 15 seconds before starting to pull out again slowly, widening the shot all the time. With your camera position near to the back of the room, you should then be able to pan slowly to look across at some of the guests who are his audience, closing in on one group or another as the shots attract you. You can partly be guided by your mental guest list. Are there any individual guests you haven't yet captured on tape, for example? But the main priority is to relate your picture to the subjects of the speech. If you know from the words of the speaker that he is about to tell a story which relates to one particular guest, or group of guests, then you need to be panning slowly across to bring them into frame as the reference is made — or as soon as possible afterwards, while they're still reacting to it. Once the speaker moves on, it's a good idea to return to him equally slowly, and to be ready for the proposal of the toast he'll make as a conclusion to his speech.

Let's now look at how this might work in the case of one speech in particular — that of the best man

An aerial view of how to cover the best man — shooting him delivering his speech from the top table and the reaction of the groom's friends, at the left-hand table, at the appropriate moment.

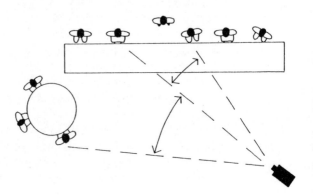

While recording the speeches, don't confine your attention to the person delivering the speech (top), but move to some of those listening (bottom), to capture their reactions to what is being said.

himself. His speech has two traditional objectives: the official aim of proposing a toast to the bridesmaids, and the unofficial, though equally traditional, aim of talking about the groom and their friendship over the years. Check with the best man beforehand if anyone else among the assembled guests will figure in his speech in addition to the groom, the bride and the bridesmaids. It may well be that another group of the groom's friends will have a major part to play in the story, for example. So, after checking the details, you know that the best man will begin by telling everyone how happy he is to see the couple married at last.

The best man's speech: pull back from the speech being delivered and pan to the couple for their reaction to his words, then back — via the best man — to the groom's schoolmates.

He'll then go on to relate a few anecdotes about the groom's past, perhaps ending on one particular story involving his former schoolmates who are also at the wedding. He will then inject a serious note into the speech by hoping they will be very happy, and he will end by praising the beauty and charm of the brides-maids, and invite everyone to drink their health, before calling on the next speaker.

Faced with this kind of plan, you can begin your recording of the speech by closing in on the best man

as he starts his delivery. Hold the close-up long enough to establish him as the source of the speech, and then begin panning to a two-shot of the bride and groom in time for the best man's references to them. When you know he's about to start telling the story of the groom's schoolmates, you can begin by panning back to the best man, then pulling out to a wider framing of the principal table, before panning slowly to find the table where one or more of the old schoolmates are sitting. Close in on them before the punch line of the story comes, so you can capture their delighted reaction, and then begin panning back to the wide shot of the principal table. Depending on how much time you feel you have left, you can then close in on the bride and groom, or return to the best man before panning back to the couple. Finally, you can return to the best man and then pan to the bridesmaids in a fairly wide shot which can also capture the proposal of the toast, and everyone else raising a drink to their health.

As speech follows speech and toast follows toast, it's also worth varying the shots which actually show the toast being drunk in each case. Not only will this help avoid repetition of similar shots, but varying the subjects and the framing as each toast is drunk will

143

give you maximum choice, and maximum opportunity for variety, when you come to edit this sequence together afterwards. By the time the speeches are finished, you should not only have a complete soundtrack of everything the speakers have said, but it should be backed by varied footage of many of the guests relaxing and enjoying themselves.

Another one of the final tasks of the best man may be to read out the greetings cards and telegrams sent by those who haven't been able to come to the wedding. Here too doing your homework is important. Some of the cards will mean more to certain groups of guests because of family or other connections, and provided you know these in advance, you can alter your picture coverage in the same way as you did for the speeches. Move slowly and carefully backwards and forwards from the best man to the guests, back to the couple — who will be interested in and pleased by all the messages — back to the best man, then back to the next group of guests, and so on through the whole succession of cards.

Covering the departure

What happens next for you as programme-maker depends on how the reception has been organised. If the couple are leaving immediately on their honeymoon, they will probably leave the room to go and change. You have the option of fading out at the end of the best man's reading of the cards — or you can continue with a few more shots of people circulating between the tables to talk to friends and relatives. This would be a way of emphasising that the formal section of the reception is over, and of capturing shots of any of the guests still missing from your programme.

Your next priority is a suitable shot, or sequence of shots, on which to end the programme. It should be clear enough to the members of your audience that the programme is reaching its conclusion, but you still need to signal this clearly enough for them not to be taken aback by the final fade-out. For example, you could fade up on the entrance of the hotel as the taxi, or the couple's own car, stands waiting for their departure. If they're travelling in their own car, the

One way of ending the programme if the couple are staying on for an evening party. Set up a romantic stroll in the hotel grounds, position them against a suitable background like a lake or a stretch of parkland, and zoom out to leave them as tiny figures in a long shot.

chances are it will have been decorated (as described in an earlier chapter) and if you're aware that this is planned, it's worth trying to shoot the process being carried out. Then you shoot the couple emerging from the hotel, running to the sanctuary of the decorated car, and driving away down the road. If this is to be your end shot, hold it as long as possible — ideally until the car has receded into a small and distant image well down the road — and then fade to black to signal the end of the programme.

If the couple are not making a departure at this stage, but are staying on for the party in the evening and leaving on their honeymoon the next day (or even later), then you have a decision to make. Would you, and they, feel happier with a mock departure along the lines described above? Apart from the fact that their leaving has been brought forward by a day, you're not really tampering with their memories of the event too much. In fact, because the token departure will be witnessed by their friends and guests, it will have more of a sense of occasion than when they genuinely leave the following day, by which time many of the guests will have left.

The alternative to staging a mock departure a day early is to stage an end shot of a different kind, but it really depends on what the location itself can offer. If, for example, the reception is being held in a country house hotel, set in its own grounds with, perhaps, a park or a lake in the background, then you can set up as elaborate a closing shot as you and the couple feel would do the programme justice. Having faded out on the end of the sequence in the reception, you could fade up again on the entrance of the hotel, either from the inside or the outside, and pick up the couple in their going-away clothes walking out of the front door, with their friends waving and wishing them well in the background. As they walk out of shot, you simply cut to a rear view of them walking away hand in hand — if not into the sunset, then into the park or down towards the lake. As the two figures diminish in your viewfinder, you can accelerate the process by zooming back slowly to end on them in a long shot — two specks in the distance setting out on their new life together — as an appropriate ending to your coverage of their wedding.

But the programme itself is far from finished. Still to come is the painstaking but creative work of post-production: turning the assembly of pictures and sound recorded during the day into a balanced and well-edited programme which will continue to surprise and delight its subjects long after the day itself has passed into the realms of memory.

Graphics and Special Effects

We shall begin the process of post-production with a look at some of the other images and ideas which can be used to advantage in the finished programme. First and foremost among these additional features is graphics — the captions and titles which give the programme an individual identity, over and above the faces of its subjects and the appearance of the locations. For example, the names of the couple, the date of their wedding, the name of the church, are all important parts of the package, and these need to be incorporated into the finished programme as smoothly as possible.

Think back first of all to the beginning of the shoot at the church. The first subjects, shot either on the recce or on the morning of the wedding day before the various guests started to arrive, were still shots of the church and its surroundings. If your camcorder has a character generator, or you have access to one which can be plugged into it, you can add the names of the couple being married and all the other details over the shots as you record them. Alternatively, it's possible to buy or hire more sophisticated character generators which can add this kind of information at the post-production stage, when you have more choice over how you build up the finished sequence over the edited shots you finally select for the programme.

However, you don't have to have character-generator facilities to be able to add titles to your programme — instead you can shoot titles and pictures together as part of the post-production process. For example, let's suggest that you take a stills camera along with you on your recce, and when you shoot the video shots of the church, the tower, the noticeboard and the spire, you shoot stills of these features as well. If you then have these pictures enlarged and printed to A3 or A4 size, you have the basis for constructing a sophisticated graphics sequence by using your camcorder as a rostrum camera.

First you need to find a suitable mounting. In many ways it's easier to record pictures using combinations of stills and graphics with the subject matter ranged horizontally, so you need to find a reliable way of mounting your camcorder vertically above the material you're shooting. There are many different ways of accomplishing this; some tripods will allow you to tilt the camcorder into the vertical position, provided you fix the feet of the tripod so that it cannot overbalance with the weight of the camcorder pulling it to one side. Individual camcorder users have improvised their own rostrum mounts from photographic enlargers, or even old drill stands. Ideally, it should be possible to move the camera and adjust it for precise positioning, but it's usually easier just to move the subject instead.

Let's now assume we have succeeded in mounting our camera vertically over a suitable flat surface (well lit on either side by a powerful lamp angled to shine down on the subject, which needs to be far enough below the camera for the lens to focus on it). If we now put the stills pictures on this flat surface, and move them so that they appear suitably framed in the viewfinder, we can record this still material in just the same way as if we were outside shooting the original. In fact, given a good sharp print and a well-lit rostrum, it would be difficult to tell the results apart — save, of course, for the lack of any movement in the scene.

Shooting a titles sequence

This now provides the basis for a titles sequence. By using a sheet of Letraset letters, and by laying them out on a clear acetate sheet, we can set up the first title to be superimposed over the first picture. There are several different ways in which this can be done in the final programme. By fixing the still picture in position and recording it for a few seconds, putting the camcorder in pause, and fixing the acetate sheet over the still before re-starting record, the title can appear as a straight cut in the finished sequence. A more time-consuming method, but one offering a smoother progression, involves shooting a time-lapse sequence with each letter in the title being edited on singly, so that the title appears to write itself across the picture. Once the full title has been on the screen long enough for the audience to take it in — allow twice the time it takes to read the words slowly — you can either edit a cut to the next picture, or peel back the acetate sheet first, keeping your hand out of shot, for a rather unusual effect. Then you place the next still picture beneath the camera, frame it up properly, prepare the next acetate sheet, and so on. You can also use other props with a rostrum camera like this, including wedding invitations and pictures from the family photograph album. We'll look at more of those in greater detail later in this chapter.

Before we leave the question of titling, however, there's another deceptively simple way of (literally) building the titles into the programme, which asks for no specialist equipment and only a little preparatory work and advance planning. This involves setting up the titles on one or more of your locations. Take, for example, the church location with which we begin the programme. If we work out our titles beforehand in terms of the names, the words and the layout, we can ask the minister's agreement to using part of his church — namely the noticeboard — as a temporary prop for our titles sequence.

It works like this: first of all you need to produce a set of title cards with the wording laid out properly. For example, the first card might say 'The wedding of . . .', and the names of the couple being married. The second card might show the date and, possibly, the time. If the layout and typeface of the letters (either hand-written or Letraset) are chosen to look as much like a printed notice as possible, these cards can be attached temporarily to the church noticeboard when you carry out the opening-sequence shoot. All you have to do is begin with, for example, a long shot of the church from the road outside, before you zoom in slowly and carefully to the noticeboard, and find the first title card occupying the frame. Having waited long enough for the audience to absorb the message,

Coping with titles — either set your camcorder up on a rostrum to shoot well-lit title cards (top) or incorporate your titles into the scenery of whatever you're shooting (bottom).

you then pull back slightly and pan to the part of the noticeboard with the second title card, and zoom back in again to pick out the title. You repeat the process with the third card and then, if you've been really careful about the timing of your shoot, you can tilt up to the church clock and show the time is right for the first guests to arrive — even if you're shooting this sequence a week before the wedding day.

You can develop a similar idea if you want to incorporate any closing titles at the end of the programme; for example a message of good wishes for the happy couple. After the closing shot of the couple driving, or walking, into the distance, you could cut to a shot of the reception table, videoed at the time when the meal was about to be served, with all the place settings in position. All you need to do is to make a set of end titles which are designed and laid out on cards similar to the place cards, the menus, or both, and position these on the table where you let the camera 'find' them, and the audience read them, one by one. The main advantage of doing titles this way is that you can develop some really ingenious ways of building them naturally into the action of the programme; amusing your audience and avoiding the need for specialist equipment to produce anything like as professional an effect.

Some techniques will call for more sophisticated equipment to create the full effect, however. Take the sequence using a selection of family-album snaps from the bride and groom's childhood and adolescent years. Using the kind of rostrum setup we were talking about earlier, it's possible to build up an entertaining and very individual sequence by simply cutting from one picture to the next. By arranging the pictures in chronological order, and in sequences of first the groom, then the bride, then the groom and then the bride, it's easy for the audience and couple to follow the life stories which finally brought them here on this day, to marry one another.

Animation techniques

There are several ways of improving on this basic sequence, though. One is to use many more pictures than the basics would call for, and edit them together snappily so the sequence is speeded up to a quite bewildering speed. The only way to decide the right pace is by trial and error, so this technique calls for experimentation. Another procedure worth bearing in mind is to change the placing of the pictures on the rostrum, and alter the zoom adjustment on the lens, so that the border of the pictures either disappears or is very obvious — but the face of the bride or groom, when young, is approximately the same size in the frame from one print to the next. When this sequence is edited quickly, you can create the illusion of a moving animation in the centre of the frame, while the outside border is changing much more quickly from shot to shot.

Another way of improving this sequence calls for the use of a special-effects generator which allows you to mix between pictures. In this case the simplest way of building up the sequence is to record all the pictures onto a second tape, which is placed in a borrowed VCR, linked, like the camcorder, to the special-effects generator (which is itself linked to the VCR on which the programme is being built up). Alternatively, if it's possible to borrow a third VCR, all you need do is record a third tape with the still pictures on, and then you can build up the sequence as before, still by still — but this time, the controls on the special-effects generator allow you to mix or dissolve from one to the other, for a much more polished sequence. Since there will be no sound associated with the still pictures, it's a good idea to pick a suitable music track — more on this in the next chapter — and edit the mixes in time with the music for a very effective introduction to the programme. This follows (or precedes) the titles and is, in turn, followed by the material shot on the wedding day itself.

There are three points worth bearing in mind when thinking about animation. If you, or your clients, feel that ending the video on a shot of the bride and the groom leaving the reception is inconclusive, then a second special-effects sequence offers a useful way out. We end the programme as we began it, with a series of still pictures to a music track. But, in this case, we are looking back instead at the wedding itself. Either you can assemble a sequence from the official stills taken by the wedding photographer or, if you have access to the right kind of special-effects equipment, you can edit together a sequence using still frames from your own video coverage. Apart from the fact that they're still pictures, the editing technique is the same as when editing together any other video shots to make the finished sequence.

You can even plump for this kind of ending to the programme if you're not able to turn your camcorder footage into still pictures. Instead, all you have to do is pick your shortest, simplest and most graphic shots, and edit them in sequence — see the next chapter — to the music track you've chosen. Keep them in the order of the day's events, and end on an especially touching shot of the bride and groom, for a neat and effective closing section to the programme.

One final word on the question of the music you use for the opening and closing sequences — or anywhere during the programme for that matter. All music is copyright, and you have to check carefully to see that you have permission to use it. One way around the problem is to use the discs or tapes released from time to time for home-movie makers, by the BBC amongst others, where copyright has been deliberately waived. In all other cases, especially if you reach the stage of being paid to make wedding videos (see Chapter Twelve) you will have to contact the Mechanical Copyright Protection Society to arrange clearance. Once this is agreed, you have access to an enormous range of library music.

10 *Editing and Dubbing*

The next stage of the post-production process centres on the different stages of editing — both picture editing and sound editing (or dubbing). This involves taking the material recorded on location and (as described in the previous chapter) on the rostrum, and arranging it to make the finished video. For most professional television programmes, this means selecting the best take of each individual shot and patching together a finished programme, edit by edit, from a mass of material many times the length of the final production.

However, we don't have the luxury of having so much material from which to choose. In some areas we may well end up with more material than is absolutely necessary; shots of the guests arriving, for instance, of people eating at the reception, or of any other sequences which are sandwiched between the main landmarks of the event, like the ceremony or the speeches. But in all the most vital sections of the programme, one take is all we have; the wedding ceremony and the speeches happen just the once, and that's the raw material from which we have to construct the best programme we can.

Having said that, editing remains a vital stage in producing a finished programme — we can still make great improvements by putting in the right cutaway over a shot which may have outstayed its welcome, or a cut which seemed to jump illogically or un-pleasingly from its predecessor. Basically, most of the editing which is done in producing a wedding video tends to involve cross-cutting backwards and for-wards between two subjects or two actions which are taking place at the same time.

Let's begin by looking at a practical example. The opening sequence, where we shot material of the bride and her family making their preparations at home, could be edited as a sequence in its own right. In that case, assuming that we are shooting the bride applying her make-up in front of a dressing-table mirror, we find a difficulty which will recur many times in the course of making a wedding video. Each of the shots, in themselves, will deal with a totally familiar and mundane subject — what makes them different is the identity of the people involved, and the romance of the occasion of their wedding. So, while we may not want to prolong a shot of someone applying make-up to the point where it becomes boring to the audience, even if they are members of the family, we don't necessarily want to imply that this is a task which is done in an instant. If we merely show a few seconds of the bride making up her face, then a couple of seconds of her brushing her hair, then a few seconds of her adjusting her veil and her headdress, we're in danger of implying that the whole elaborate process of the bride getting ready for her wedding is something rushed and breathless. Yet if we prolong this sequence in the context of the whole programme, we risk the rest of the video becoming a confusing blur.

This is where editing comes in. Let's look at the make-up shot once again. All we really need of that shot is the bride starting to apply her make-up, and then applying the finishing touches. What comes in between is so totally familiar that it's not needed at all. But if we simply showed her starting to apply her make-up, then cut straight to her finishing the task, the result would give us a jump cut. The make-up would suddenly seem to have applied itself to her face, a suggestion which the audience would find confusing and amateurish.

So one option is to look for a cutaway — a picture on the bedside table perhaps — which we can cut to after showing the bride starting to apply her make-up. Then we cut back to the bride finishing her task, and the jump cut is avoided. So far so good; there will certainly be times when editing in a cutaway shot offers the only solution to this problem. But the number of potential cutaways around the house will be limited, and many of them won't really be ideal. By their very nature they're often static, so they slow down the pace of the whole sequence. And, if the audience becomes aware that you're repeatedly showing them a shot of a task being started, a static cutaway, a shot of the task being finished, they will find the pictures monotonous and uninspiring. This response will be evoked despite all the care you may have taken to frame them properly, to vary the angles and the type of shot used, and to look for unexpected or unusual glimpses of familiar subjects.

One way to solve this problem is, first, to look for cut-aways which relate directly to what we've just been looking at, rather than something which just happens to be in the same room. In the case of the make-up example, a cutaway of various cosmetics arrayed on the dressing table would have been a better idea, for although it's still a static subject, it does at least have something to do with what we've just seen happening. Even better would have been a shot of one of the bridesmaids waiting for her turn in front of the mirror, and clearly watching the bride's efforts with close attention. In both these cases we're still cutting away from the bride's face, so that we don't suddenly find the task has been miraculously finished in the cut from one shot to the next. However, we're not cutting so far away that there's the danger of the cutaway shot appearing irrelevant, and the cut back to the make-up being finished becoming a different kind of distraction.

The importance of cross-cutting

Unfortunately, as you'll find when shooting this sequence, varied and directly related cutaways are

The bride putting on her make-up: cut away to something else to avoid the shot lasting too long, and only return when she's finished, or when someone else has taken her place.

scarce and hard to find in every case. This is where cross-cutting comes in. Your audience is going to accept that while the bride is applying her make-up, other people are having to rush to get ready too — the bride's father for one, the bride's mother for another, and any of the bridesmaids, pages and attendants who may be staying at the house, or who may be using the bride's home as a place to change into their outfits and depart for the church.

We'll cover the mechanics of editing different shots together to build up the finished programme later in this chapter. For the time being, we'll simply consider how the different shots are placed in order when assembling the programme sequences. For example, let's return for a moment to our bride, applying her make-up in front of the dressing-table mirror. At the time that she's absorbed in this task, her father may well be fastening his collar and knotting his tie in front of another mirror in the sitting room. Even if these tasks don't take place at exactly the same moment on the day, the audience is going to be perfectly happy to accept that they *might* have happened at the same time, so that cross-cutting between them becomes perfectly feasible.

This gives us the opportunity of cutting from our first shot of the bride starting to apply make-up, to a shot of her father downstairs fastening his collar, looking down to pick up his tie and turning to the mirror. We cut to another shot looking at his face in the mirror as he starts to knot his tie, which then gives us the opportunity of cutting back to the bride applying the finishing touches to her make-up. As she stands up for a bridesmaid to take her place and apply her own make-up, we can then cut back to the father, who is tightening his tie and beginning to comb his hair. From this point we can cut to any other shot of the bride, even if we stay with her father while she comes downstairs to show that she's now almost ready. The result is that two difficult sequences have worked perfectly well through cross-cutting, without using any cutaways at all. Of course, if we're lucky enough to have cutaways which actually add to the variety of the sequences (the bridesmaids watching the bride as they wait for their turn in front of the mirror, the bride's mother looking around the door to see if her husband is ready yet) then editing these into the sequence makes it still more varied and well-balanced. What's important, though, is that we can now consider whether or not to include cutaways on their own merits as attractive or appropriate shots, and not simply to prevent potential jump cuts intruding into our sequences.

This principle of cross-cutting can be extended still further. If, in addition to shooting the preparations at the home of the bride, we also recorded sequences showing the groom and the best man putting on their wedding outfits and leaving for the church, this offers a second opportunity for cross-cutting — with the even more appropriate bonus that we can cut backwards and forwards between the two stars of our programme. After a shot of the bride with her make-up, we now have the opportunity of seeing the groom washing, shaving and putting on his tie, or combing his hair, and so on.

The more ambitious type of cross-cutting also gives us an opportunity for some comparison and contrast shots. If, when we view the material, we find that all is panic and chaos at the groom's home, compared with the unruffled calm at the bride's house, then this contrast can be shown very powerfully indeed by the way you order the shots. Alternatively, you may prefer to pick out the similarities; a shot of the bride's father giving her a fond glance as she shows him the full wedding outfit, and a shot of the groom's mother straightening his tie and brushing his jacket, seen consecutively, will strike a chord with the audience and lend a little extra style to your programme.

Editing location material

What about editing our shots together when all the action is taking place at a single location, for example at the church? When events are happening in very quick succession, such as the arrival of the guests who are all basically doing the same thing, walking past you and the camera and straight into the church, then cutaways are likely to be almost impossible. What's needed here is as much variety as possible in terms of the subjects of your shots, the angles from which you shot them, and the framing you used. The more viewpoints and compositions you were able to bring to bear in shooting similar groups of people all following one another up a path and through a doorway, the easier the editing will be, without any danger of jump cuts or clumsy transitions. In fact, if any cuts do prove problematic, the best way to overcome the difficulty is simply to rearrange the sequence which shows the guests arriving into a different order.

This may well solve the problem without anyone watching the programme being aware of the slight tampering which had to be done to make the pictures fit. But what happens when you come to the service itself? In this case, you are more restricted to the material you recorded, in the order in which you recorded it, as it depended on the order of the pronouncements by the minister and the responses from the couple. You can only hope that your fade-outs and fade-ins allowed you to capture the highlights, while your recording of the formal vows by the bride and groom will have an immediacy of their own which more than makes up for the length of the shot, or the amount of time you needed to keep to the same framing while the words were being spoken. If, however, you find there are some parts of the service which are less important, and which you only recorded as an insurance policy, these can be cut at the editing stage. The shots they contain can, in some cases, be used as extra cutaways for the sections you keep in the finished programme.

When you are outside again, for the photographic session, it's a case of returning to cross-cutting as a way of keeping the material varied, injecting a sense of pace, and avoiding uncomfortable jumps in the transition from shot to shot. This is the reason for alternating shots of the groups being assembled and photographed with shots of the surroundings (either the other guests watching, or the photographer going through his routine). Cuts to one or other of these subjects will bridge the gaps between a particular group being assembled and the actual picture being taken, which would otherwise drag the shot out far too long for comfort. Instead the shot of a group (for example the couple with their respective parents) can be recorded as the group assembles, with perhaps a wide shot and a series of close-ups and two-shots as

A registry-office wedding — smaller, less ceremonial and easier to cover.

162

they begin to get in line and face the camera. To avoid the apparently interminable wait for the photographer to get the picture as he wants it, before he presses the shutter, a shot of some of the onlookers is edited in. This is then followed by a shot of the photograph being taken and a shot of the group relaxing from the formal pose, and perhaps dissolving into laughter. The result is a varied and entertaining sequence from something as routine (in wedding terms) as the taking of a formal photograph.

We move on now to the reception. Here the problem in editing is similar to that which we encountered in compiling the sections shot in the church. The sequences with the speeches were recorded in full, so that nothing was missed out, and this restricts the way in which this section can be assembled for the programme. Once again, the most which can be attempted is to use any cutaways of the room — close-ups of the guests listening to the speeches, glasses being raised and drunk from, pieces of wedding cake being passed to the guests, or anything else you may have had time to shoot over and above recording the speeches themselves — to help break the long moving shot which covers each speech, and to help the sequence seem like a normally edited programme segment.

By now it should be clear that the demands and restrictions of shooting and editing a wedding video set it apart from most other kinds of programme. So much of the subject matter (all the most important sections) has to be captured in full, as it happens. This means that cutaways in these sections, while still desirable, become something of a luxury — unless you can find the time to shoot them when the bulk of your material is safely recorded. It also means that the pace of events prevents you from adopting the normal technique of shooting a subject, and then moving to capture it from a different position and a different angle, in all except a few cases where your subjects will stay in place long enough for you to do this. Hence the need for cross-cutting between two different subjects, and actions, which are happening at the same time, or which the audience will accept are happening at the same time.

Constructing a sequence

In all other respects, however, the normal rules of editing apply. Let's assume that you are building up a sequence from a mass of material you have shot during the taking of the wedding photographs. You choose, as your first shot in the sequence, the couple walking out of the church to be greeted by the photographer. You need to copy enough of this shot from the tape in the camcorder onto the programme tape which you are assembling in the VCR, so that the audience can understand exactly what is happening. So the question you need to ask is, for how long does the shot have something interesting to say?

It may be that the shot captures the photographer walking up to the couple and persuading them to move to where he wants them to pose for the picture. If all this happens reasonably smoothly, you could copy it over to this point and then look for another shot to edit after it. But if there's a long pause while they stand and wait for the photographer to tell them what he wants, the shot becomes static and boring. In this case you need to copy just enough of it to show the audience that the newly-wed couple have now emerged from the church, and that the photographs are about to be taken.

What should your next shot be? If the first one lasted long enough to follow the photographer and the couple away from the church door, then we can cut back to some of the other guests watching the first picture being taken. As long as you can see these guests coming out of the door — or provided your framing on them is so tight that you can't see the door at all — the audience will assume they emerged while the photographer was talking to the couple. If, on the other hand, the shot can only be used up to the point where the couple pause and wait for instructions, then we haven't yet seen the photographer, so the best shot to edit next would be a reverse shot of the photographer calling instructions to them. This could then be followed by a shot of some of the guests watching — since the audience will assume they have followed the couple out of the church while we were looking at the photographer, and so on.

Once you are safely into the sequence the choice of shots available should be easier, as you can cut quite freely between the photographer, the people whose picture he is taking, and the other guests. Here the overriding objective should be to maintain a rhythm from shot to shot and from subject to subject, without forgetting about the basic rules of editing. Don't record too much of any shot onto your programme tape, beyond the point at which it becomes static and predictable. By all means record more than you need as a safety margin but, when positioning your next edit, find the point at which you think the previous shot should end so that it is cut back accordingly.

Also, try not to cut out in the middle of a decisive movement by your subject — if they turn round, or walk out of frame, end that shot on the start of the movement or after it's finished. (Smaller and more repetitive movements don't pose the same problem; a shot of someone waving to someone else out of

Setting up your camcorder (1) and VCR (4) for editing in post-production. Connections are from the output of camcorder (2) to the VIDEO-IN connection of VCR (3), with a separate cable linking VCR to TV (5).

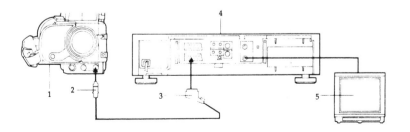

frame can be cut wherever you like.) You also need to avoid cutting out of a shot in the middle of a camera movement like a pan, tilt, zoom, or change-focus. Either wait until the movement has finished, cut before it starts, or use a different shot altogether.

It's better to avoid a cut from a subject to another shot with the same subject in part of the frame, since there is a danger of a jump cut. It's better if the subjects are completely different (though part of the same overall context) and, in an ideal world, the edit will work better if the camera angle and the framing is different as well. Finally, the very best edits will keep the main focus of interest in the same area of the frame, so that the eyes of the audience focus on it naturally, and the edit appears smooth and unobtrusive as all good edits should. You won't always be able to meet all these requirements in the context of covering a wedding, as easily as you would in a carefully paced and scripted production fully under your control as director, but you should at least be aware of them. If an edit doesn't appear jarring and uncomfortable, then it's a pretty good edit; but if you don't feel comfortable about a particular cut between one shot and the next, try to rearrange the sequence or use a different shot to avoid the problem. Sometimes three shots which make for two awkward cuts, when assembled in one particular order, can edit together beautifully if the order is changed — or if a particular shot is lengthened or shortened to give a different cutting point.

Sound dubbing

One of the supreme advantages of video, as opposed to film, is that you always have synchronised sound on your tape — depending on what was actually recorded through the microphone. But covering the important parts of the wedding — in sound terms as well as visuals — almost inevitably means more than one sound input. At the very least you'll have one microphone providing all the important foreground sound for the responses in the church and for the speeches at the reception, and another (usually the camera microphone) recording background sound for general atmosphere. You may also want to have a music track over parts of the tape, so this adds another degree of complexity. How can you mix and match these different sounds within the limited channels available to you on the video cassette, without spending a fortune on audio equipment or hiring special facilities to carry out the job?

Let's answer that by looking a little more closely at how sound is recorded onto video cassettes. Although VHS, S-VHS (and their compact versions), Video 8 and Hi8 formats all have two sound channels — which allow the recording and playback of stereo sound or two individual sound channels on the right equipment — some camcorders will only effectively allow you to record a single sound channel. This means that, as you record sound and vision when you shoot, the sound is determined by whatever is picked up by the camera microphone at the time. If you connect an auxiliary microphone to the camcorder as well as the standard microphone, the camcorder will record the sound picked up by the auxiliary microphone, effectively switching off the standard fixture. The only way to record sound from two separate inputs on this type of machine would be to connect the leads from two microphones into a simple audio mixer. This will have a single output lead for connection into the auxiliary microphone socket on the camcorder.

As far as wedding videos are concerned, this kind of arrangement may give you the flexibility you need to cope with most of the sound-dubbing requirements of the programme. For example, the sequences of the bride and groom preparing to leave for the church, the guests arriving for the ceremony, the minister conducting the service, the bride and groom saying

167

the responses, the taking of the official photographs and the speeches and toasts at the reception, all could be edited with the sound from the original camera tapes going with the pictures as a single edit. Provided you adjust the sound level at each edit so the volume of the soundtrack doesn't go up and down too sharply (which depends, of course, on how close you were to the source of sound in each particular shot), the results should be quite acceptable as a sound-and-vision record of the day's events.

There are only two areas where you may meet with problems. One is any special-effects, or pre-title, sequence where you want to edit a series of stills, or moving pictures for that matter, over a music track. In this case, you will need to ensure the VCR you use for editing the programme will permit you to dub a soundtrack onto one of the audio channels of your master cassette. You can do this by connecting an audio cassette recorder, or CD player, to the audio-dub input of your VCR, and simply copying over the required amount of music to cover your intended sequence. It will take a certain amount of pre-planning to decide the length your sequence will be once the pictures are put on, and you need to fade up the recording level at the start of your music extract and fade it down again at the end. But, once done, you'll have a very effective blueprint for your picture edit. All you need do to make the most of the music track is to ensure you edit your pictures in time to the music, and your sequence will have an inherent rhythm of its own.

You may, however, find that your VCR will only allow you to dub an audio track onto an existing picture sequence, so that as you edit your pictures onto the tape, the soundtrack progressively disappears. In that case, you have two options — once the pictures are in place, you can re-record the sound as an audio dub to finish the job, or you can simply time the piece of music you want to use, making a note of the timings of the natural cutting points, and edit the pictures on without the music, adding the music afterwards. But this is a very laborious way of achieving the same result, and a method which will all too easily allow errors to creep in.

The second potential problem area concerns those all-important sequences — the responses in the church and the speeches at the reception — where you've recorded the action as one long shot in order to preserve the vital soundtrack. So long as you edit these long-lasting shots onto your programme tape as one complete sound-and-vision sequence, no problem arises. But where you have some cutaway shots which you want to copy onto your programme tape to relieve the monotony of the endless single shot, without interrupting the soundtrack, you need to proceed with caution. Make sure it's possible to edit these shots over the existing sequence without erasing the original soundtrack. If this is difficult, or impossible, it might be better to forget about the possibility of using cutaways during these sequences altogether.

In the end, whatever the capabilities and limitations of your camcorder and VCR, as far as audio dubbing and editing are concerned, there is one particular piece of additional equipment which is invaluable in helping to assemble a professional and polished programme — and that's an audio mixer. Simple audio mixers, as we explained earlier, allow you to mix the input from different microphones onto a single audio channel for recording onto the tape. But the more sophisticated models can be used at the editing stage to allow you to blend together several different sound inputs — your original sound from the camera tape on one or two channels (one for foreground sound, one for atmosphere, for example) a music track and even, for some programme subjects, a voice-over commentary. All of these can be mixed and balanced in the right proportions through the mixer, for recording onto one or two audio channels on the finished programme tape.

The final checks

By the time the soundtrack has been mixed and dubbed — or assembled shot by shot as described earlier — your programme is well on the way to completion. As the editing and dubbing is taking place, in some cases shot by shot and in other areas sequence by sequence, you have a chance to monitor the overall balance of the programme. Is its length running close enough to your intended running time of between 60 and 90 minutes? Is the amount of time devoted to the ceremony, or the reception, about right? Have you devoted enough time to the less important features of the day — like the photographs — or do those sequences last far too long for their relative importance? And have you included shots of all the key people the couple will expect to see in their wedding video?

At this stage you can't go back and shoot anything you may have missed on the vital day — but if you have the material safely shot, and the length of the programme and the balance between its different sections needs changing, the edit gives you the chance to correct these defects. With a little more time and trouble it is still possible to refine and improve the programme you make from the material you recorded. Putting in that extra effort now will not only bring you extra pleasure from the delight your audience will take in the results, it will also help to ensure your next wedding video is even better, because of all you've learned in making this one.

We've now reached the end of the process involved in making a straightforward wedding video, based on a traditional Church of England service and a conventional reception. Although we've tried to cover most of the questions which might arise in making a wedding programme against this background, we need to remember that there are other kinds of weddings which differ to a greater or lesser extent from this norm. There are registry-office weddings, Roman Catholic, Nonconformist, Jewish and Orthodox Church weddings, let alone the Hindu, Moslem and Chinese varieties. In the next chapter, we shall look at some of the more common variations from the routine which we have used as the basis for our coverage, and at the different challenges and opportunities these present for the video programme-maker.

We've also covered the subject from the viewpoint of a video enthusiast coming to terms with making a video programme on a single wedding in particular — as a favour to friends, or as a new challenge in terms of using the equipment to make an entertaining, popular and well-made programme. But what happens if the results of your efforts are so successful, to you as well as to your audience, that you're tempted to repeat the process over and over again, covering other people's weddings on a commercial, or even a semi-commercial, basis?

The do's and don'ts are still much the same, but in order to make the whole exercise viable, you will need to evolve a routine which will allow you to use your increasing experience to the full, while keeping the whole operation as controlled, and as efficient, as possible. You will need to become more adept at pricing, and at assessing the difficulties in different clients' requirements. You will need to consider hiring extra help, to carry equipment and assist with the lighting and the microphone cables. You will need to think about buying more equipment to make your job easier, and to enable you to produce more polished results, without having to take so much time and effort that the whole exercise becomes uneconomic. We shall cover all these points, from buying additional equipment to hints on advertising and marketing, in the closing chapter of this book.

Different Kinds of Weddings

So far we've been looking at the task of making a wedding video against the background of what is probably still the most common type of wedding to be made the subject of a video programme — a church service, followed by a reception at a pub, a hotel or a restaurant. But this is still only one type of wedding, in terms of the location and the order of events which you have to try to capture. What difference will it make, from you as the video programme-maker's point of view, if the wedding you find yourself shooting is one that differs in some way from this norm?

Let's begin with those closest to the routine we've been covering. Generally speaking, other church and chapel weddings in Britain will differ very little from the kind of ceremony we've been describing — in terms of the order of the service and the kind of location which provides the background — and the receptions associated with them will vary hardly at all. Roman Catholic weddings, for example, may well involve a nuptial mass, which is a church service in addition to the ritual of the wedding itself. There may also be an optional part of the ceremony which involves the exchanging of rings between bride and groom but, in terms of the shots you will want to capture and the problems of doing them justice, these changes present only differences in detail rather than exerting a major effect on what you hope to achieve. All you need to remember is to check out the precise form of service with the couple, and find out which parts of it — in addition to their vows and responses — they would like you to record in full.

In one respect, recording Roman Catholic weddings can be easier than recording Church of England services, the reason being simply that many Catholic parish priests are more relaxed about the ceremony being recorded in the church than their Anglican opposite numbers. But this can vary from place to place, and in all cases you need to do your best to reassure the minister, or the priest, of your willingness to be guided by them in terms of access, camera positions and the possibility of deploying microphones or background lighting.

Nonconformist chapels, too, can offer distinct advantages over many Anglican churches. All too often the traditional village church, while looking absolutely beautiful, and highly appropriate as a background for a romantic occasion like a wedding, from the outside, can be distinctly dark and gloomy on the inside. Chapels — particularly the more modern ones — are often lighter and smaller, freeing you from the need for lights and making your microphone requirements simpler and less time-consuming to set up.

Registry-office weddings

Oddly enough, the non-religious wedding ceremony — in a registry office rather than a church or chapel — has been known to present real difficulties. At one time it was generally very difficult indeed to persuade registrars to give permission to record the ceremony on video, although this does seem to be changing. If you do strike lucky, and you find you are able to shoot within the registry office itself, it makes an ideal location in many ways. It's usually a well-lit and compact room, with no sound or lighting problems, and you can be close enough to the couple and their witnesses (these weddings require two witnesses rather than a best man and bridesmaid, though in many cases the roles are combined) to hear and record everything they say.

The ritual itself is different from the church wedding. To begin with, it's shorter and simpler, although the couple do have to repeat vows (prompted by the official who conducts the service), and then they and the witnesses sign the register on the spot. This gives you another important part of the wedding to record, without having to worry about moving to another location, and perhaps missing out on a later part of the action. Suitable subjects for cutaways may not be so plentiful, though some registry offices have pictures and flower arrangements which might solve the problem for you. On the other hand, as the ceremony is a brief one, you shouldn't need so much in the way of cutaway material in the first place.

As far as photographs are concerned, these will have to be shot outside the office once the ceremony is over. Depending on the location of the office, this may well not give you the kind of photogenic background a church would provide — the same may well be true of chapels, particularly those in towns rather than in the country — so you would be better advised to record this part of the proceedings as simply as possible, and to try to capture more shots of the couple and their guests after they arrive at the reception, where time and space will be more plentiful and you can go for more varied shots.

Sometimes the choice may not be a clear-cut one between a religious and a secular service — you may actually encounter a little of both. It's becoming increasingly popular, where one or both partners have been married before, to have a registry-office wedding with a blessing performed in a church. In this case, you should find out as much as you can beforehand, not only in terms of the order in which the events will take place, but also the form the blessing will take, and what the couple themselves want to have recorded in detail (provided of course you can have permission to do so).

In all cases we have assumed that the reception itself will probably follow the routine we have described earlier, a welcome drink or two, a meal served at the table or as a buffet, followed by the cutting of the cake, a set of speeches by specified individuals, and the reading of the cards. But different people have different traditions, which may well affect your priorities in capturing as much of the reality as possible. It's quite common in Italian weddings, for example, for the relatives or guests to stand up and deliver a speech as the mood takes them, which makes it difficult to record them properly. All you can do in this kind of situation is even more careful homework; in terms of finding out who is likely to speak (and where they will be sitting), what they're likely to say, what order they're likely to say it in, and how long they will take to say it — and it's still worth being on your guard for the completely unexpected!

Shooting a Greek wedding

The other half of the Christian church — the Orthodox Church — takes in areas of the world like Russia and Eastern Europe, as well as Greece and eastern parts of the Mediterranean. As their rituals, and even in some cases their calendar, differ from that used in Western Europe, it's hardly surprising that wedding ceremonies diverge quite considerably from their Anglican, Roman Catholic and Nonconformist counterparts. In fact, the differences within an essentially similar overall ceremony present both a challenge and an opportunity for the video producer, provided you can search out sufficient information beforehand.

At a Greek wedding the differences start before the ceremony itself; the preparations at the homes of the bride and groom involve traditions which are very much worth capturing if you can. At the groom's house the finishing touches will be added to his wedding outfit by the best man, while the family watch and sing traditional songs, often accompanied by a musician playing the fiddle. Finally, before the groom leaves for the church, a dish containing burning incense is passed three times around his head by each of the principal guests.

In the meantime (though you'll have to ask for a certain amount of cheating on the precise timing to be able to shoot at both locations, especially if they are some distance apart) a similar ritual will be carried out at the bride's home. In this case, final adjustments are made to her headdress while a fiddler plays traditional Greek music, and, once again a dish of burning incense is passed three times around her head by each of the guests, before she leaves for the church and the ceremony.

At the church, two differences from the Western ritual are immediately apparent: the guests light candles as they arrive, buttonholes are distributed, and when the couple themselves arrive they enter the church together. In fact the groom arrives with the bride's bouquet, which he hands to her before they enter the church, the groom leading, the bride following. From that point onwards, all the guests gather round them for the service, which means you either need to arrange for a gap to be left, or you need permission to shoot from a vantage point high up enough to capture what's happening over the heads of friends, family and relatives.

The routine of the service is different too. The priest blesses the couple with a long ribbon (which plays an important part later in the ritual), he then turns his back on them and continues the service, while the guests all offer the couple their congratulations. The priest then blesses two circlets of beads, before turning to the couple and placing these circlets on their heads.

At this point the chief bridesmaid takes one end of the ribbon and fastens it to the bride's dress, before passing it round the congregation for the guests to write their names on it. The best man then picks up a wine glass which he passes to the priest, who gives it to the groom and then to the bride. Finally, the ribbon is rewound before being pinned to the groom, and then removed, and the priest takes the groom's hand and leads the bridal party three times round the table from which he conducted the service, with the guests each slapping the groom on the back as they pass by.

After the service is over, the guests each kiss the priest's Bible before kissing the bride and groom. The couple then sign the register before — another difference from the Western routine — the guests leave the church in advance of them. This allows them to get into the best possible position for showering the couple with confetti as they emerge through the church door and rush for the safety of the car taking them to the reception. It also gives you sufficient time to move outside the church with the guests to make the most of this colourful, but fast-moving, scene.

Even the reception has its individual features. Instead of the formal receiving line of a typical Anglican wedding, the couple enter the room where the reception is to be held and walk round the dance floor three times, followed by the children among the wedding guests, before they take their seats for the meal to begin. When the meal is over the dancing (usually a mixture of modern and traditional Greek) begins. The couple will lead the first waltz, and as the guests join in they pass them presents by pinning banknotes and cheques to their clothes.

Shooting a Jewish wedding

If it is possible to have so many detailed differences between one type of Christian wedding and another, then it should hardly be surprising that a Jewish wedding will have even more special features you will need to be aware of before planning your shoot. For example, when the bride arrives at the synagogue she will go to a special room set aside as the bride's room, with the groom's mother and her own mother. The groom, meanwhile, will sign the casooba (the Jewish wedding certificate) before the service begins. As with the Catholic church, it is quite common for an afternoon service, called the Mincha, to be held before the wedding service proper. And although it isn't usually essential for you to shoot this part of the service unless you have been specifically asked to do so, it does offer a good chance to capture footage of many of the guests if you can do it unobtrusively. In fact, at this stage of the service it will probably be acceptable for you to move about the synagogue quite freely — but, as always, check this beforehand.

Once the Mincha is over the actual wedding service begins. The groom, his father, the bride's father, the best man and the rabbi who will perform the ceremony join the bride and the mothers of the couple in the bride's room for what is called the bedecking; the final preparations before the ceremony starts. After the bedecking, the groom and the best man return and stand under a canopy, called a chuppah, where the ceremony will take place. The bride and the rest of the wedding party then emerge from the bride's room to join them, sometimes with the mothers and the groom's father walking down the aisle behind the bride and her father.

The rest of the wedding takes place under the chuppah, which poses two problems from your point of view in covering the proceedings. One problem is that the chuppah itself may get in the way, and it will certainly cut down the light level where you need it most. Secondly, you will probably find that the rabbi tends to block your view when you want to shoot what's happening — so have a word before the service begins to arrange a gap between the rabbi and the rest of the guests so you can see, and shoot, what is happening.

The ritual itself is fairly involved and is usually conducted in Hebrew, so check with the couple about the parts they specifically want included — like the bride walking round the groom seven times, and like the couple drinking a toast from a glass which the groom then places on the floor and breaks. At moments like this, you'll have to take all the care you can that the congregation, in its desire to see as much as possible of what is happening, doesn't obstruct your view.

Then, as with a Christian wedding, comes the signing of the register. In this case, it usually takes place on a platform, called the bimah, in the centre of the synagogue — rather than in a separate vestry. But even so, you may find it difficult to get a clear view of the proceedings unless you choose your position carefully. Another point worth bearing in mind is that at this stage the congregation itself is probably making quite a lot of noise, so, if your camcorder permits, you can turn down your audio level, as the scene you're shooting is almost entirely visual. Once the register is signed, it's usual for the couple to be shown into the bride's room and locked in there for a few minutes.

Not all the differences are confined to the ceremony. Although the majority of Jewish wedding receptions are similar to the receptions we covered earlier in the book, they do tend to be longer and more formal — so that once again you need to agree your precise objectives with the couple for whom you're making the video.

For example, they'll probably want you to shoot the opening of the reception — when all the guests are seated, the couple walk in to take their places, to loud applause from all present. From then on, however, the speeches tend to be longer, and there are more of them, than is common at the receptions covered earlier. In many cases there may be speeches from representatives of organisations with which the families are involved, as well as from various members of the families themselves. There will often be two loyal toasts — one to the Queen and one to the President of Israel — and a grace will be said after the meal rather than before it. As this is very long, check whether the couple want it all recorded or whether the first couple of verses would be sufficient. The grace is usually followed by a series of seven blessings, called the Sheva Brochos, and they are much more likely to want these filmed in full.

Perhaps the biggest difference between a Jewish reception and our earlier example, is that the dinner itself is a much more important part of the proceedings, and it's acceptable to show more footage of the guests eating and the meal in progress than you might normally do. Finally, when the meal is over and the dancing begins, it's usual for the bride and groom to be carried shoulder-high by their friends, making for a noisy and spectacular rounding-off to your video coverage of the day.

The commonalities

From these two examples, it's clear that different cultures and different traditions produce totally different versions of the wedding ceremony and of the reception. Once we begin to consider wedding traditions from further afield — Hindu, Sikh, Muslim, and Chinese weddings (which often incorporate an elaborate tea ceremony) — the picture becomes impossibly complex.

But some points still hold good. No matter what kind of tradition, or what part of the world it originates from, determine in advance the shape of the wedding you intend to cover. Remember to find out all the information you can first, do your planning and recce carefully, and always take the utmost trouble to find out what your couple wants to see in their wedding video. Pick out the parts which are important enough to need covering in their entirety, and approach them as we approached the shoot of the vows and responses in the church and the speeches at the reception. In all other cases, remember to shoot the highlights, go for as many reaction shots and cut-aways as you can, and build up a rhythm of shooting. When you edit the programme together afterwards, keep cross-cutting between different shots and subjects to maintain the pace, and keep the visuals interesting.

It's also possible to start and finish the programme, whatever the form of the wedding and the reception, with the creative treatments we suggested as possibilities for a Western wedding. You could start off the programme by building up a music-and-stills sequence, based on the childhood and adolescence of the couple (taken from the family snapshot album), then construct a similar music-and-stills recapitulatory section to round off the programme, using stills taken by the official wedding photographer. If there isn't one, or if you're not very pleased with the choice, use pictures selected from your own coverage edited together as a quick sequence in chronological order — from the start of the preparations to the end of the reception, as we explained in the chapter on graphics and special effects. What's most important in the coverage of any wedding, anywhere in the world, is that it should convey a happy and romantic occasion, and the gift you're bringing to the couple with your programme is a secure and completely non-perishable record of their very special day. Keep that aim firmly in mind, from the start of your planning to the final edit and the showing of the finished programme, and you can't go wrong.

Commercial
Wedding Videos

One of the most intriguing features of the wedding video, as opposed to the video of the family holiday, of the children growing up, or of all the usual subjects that are recorded by the home-video enthusiast, is that it has a potential commercial value. All over the country, companies and individual enthusiasts all offering couples and their families the chance of paying to have a programme made of their wedding — in exactly the same way as has been outlined during the course of this book. So, for anyone who has followed the advice given, who has made one or more wedding-video programmes for friends or relatives, and who has both enjoyed the challenge and found that the results have been well appreciated, an interesting question emerges — what are the possibilities of doing the same thing for other people, on a regular commercial basis?

The first point to be aware of, long before taking any decision on the matter, is that covering a wedding for the first time involves a lot more time and effort than would be economical as a way of earning a living. If you actually added up all the time spent researching, recceing and planning, shooting on the previous day and on the day of the wedding itself, and editing and dubbing afterwards, then costed it as the equivalent proportion of a reasonable week's pay, the total price at the end of the day would be far above the market rate, and would almost certainly involve no profit margin at all.

On the other hand, there is a very powerful learning process involved. One of the factors which should have been clear from the descriptions in the book is that weddings, as subjects for video programmes, have a lot more important things in common, whatever the kind of wedding we may be considering, than they have individual differences. So each successive wedding video you make is helping you with the learning process. The more familiar you become with the order of events, with the ritual of the ceremony, and with the way in which receptions are planned and conducted, the less daunting a challenge the whole task will become. The less you have to worry about what exactly comes next, the quicker you will be to react to what *does* happen in terms of the unusual, the unexpected, and the unheralded change of plan which demands that you think on your feet. Once you reach that stage, two things will happen. Your programmes will become more spontaneous, and more individual (exactly the qualities needed) and you'll have to contribute less time and energy as an insurance policy against your own inexperience.

Costing and pricing

The result of this learning process is that you will become more efficient, and more economical in terms of the cost to you (the time and effort you have to put into making the programme), which means you can price your wedding video at something closer to the current market rate. At present this varies quite widely depending on the person offering the service, from the thoroughly professional (in terms of approach, as we said earlier, rather than simply whether or not a fee is charged) videographer to the paid amateur seeking to earn a little bit of extra money on the side.

It is possible to have a video made of your wedding for as little as between £90 and £150, and people pricing their efforts at this level are relying on two factors in their favour. Many people not experienced in shooting video themselves still have surprisingly low expectations of the record of their wedding — if they can see, and recognise, themselves, their families, friends and the occasion, they may very well be delighted. They may not notice, or worry about, the amateur camera work and the sloppy standards of production, at least at first. Even if they do, the wedding market is one where, for obvious reasons, there is almost no repeat business. Your clients are your clients for the one and only programme you make of their wedding and, if they're not pleased, it's all too easy for a cowboy operator to find new customers who may not realise, until it's too late, what they will actually get for their money.

The final point of all your planning and preparation: your clients sitting down to re-live their great day through the images you've preserved for them on tape.

A more realistic price, for a good wedding video, would be from £300 upwards — depending on the degree of complexity involved. People who have a very clear idea of the extra sequences and polished special effects they want to see in their own personal wedding video may be prepared to pay more — up to around £1,000 in some cases. But it's extremely likely that such demanding customers would do a great deal of shopping around before commissioning someone to do the job, and they would want to see some samples of work. It would be better to consider

beginning at the lower end of the price scale, until both your work and your reputation become firmly established.

Market limitations

If this way of earning money sounds tempting, it's essential to be aware of some factors which limit your potential market, and the overall earnings you could expect from making wedding videos. First of all, producing wedding videos on a serious basis does call for a good deal of equipment, over and above a decent personal camcorder. The more features your camcorder has, and the better its low-light performance, the easier it will be to use as part of a capable and reliable editing system. You'll need extra features like a character generator to superimpose titles on the picture, and you'll need extra microphones — possibly even radio microphones if you're really serious — with a sound mixer to produce really high quality, well-balanced soundtracks.

Secondly, the nature of the wedding market itself creates other limitations on the return you can expect from it. The majority of weddings in Britain tend to take place on Saturdays. This limits your earning days to 52 per year at the most — and, in fact, the potential is a lot less as the wedding market tends to be seasonally biased towards the spring, the summer and the early autumn months. You *might* be able to tackle two weddings in a single day, but the opportunities where the locations and the timings are going to make that possible will be very limited, and in such cases the extra money will certainly be well-earned!

Another problem is that people wanting to arrange a wedding very often have to book the church and the reception more than a year ahead, if they want to be sure of arranging the event on the date they prefer. While they may be willing to book their wedding video a little nearer the day itself, it's quite likely they will want to have everything tied up well in advance. This means you will have to commit your time a long way ahead — and stick to your schedule no matter what other pressures or pleasures might intervene.

The third problem with the wedding-video market was mentioned earlier, in passing, and that is its non-repeatability factor. In all other areas of professional video production, the greatest incentive to make a polished and attractive programme is to keep the client happy, for a happy client is not just a customer for the production in progress, but may well be the source of future commissions too. Not so with wedding videos. If you turn out an absolutely first-class production for a particular couple, they will probably be delighted with your work, and be very grateful for the effort you put in. They may feel your work has been fairly priced, and they may feel the decision to ask you to do the job, rather than your competitors, was the best they could have made. What they *won't* be able to do is give you another job, since if their marriage turns out to be all they hope it will be, the event won't be repeated — and certainly not inside any kind of sensible timescale.

Advertising and marketing

All you can hope, with happy and satisfied customers for one of your programmes, is that the couple involved will tell their friends. If other couples in their group are planning to marry, they may well have seen your programme — as part of the audience outside the immediate family — and they may already know what kind of production you can deliver. If the couple for whom you made the programme tell them about the price, and how careful you were to find out what they wanted and to take their wishes into account as far as possible, this is a powerful incentive for them to book you to do the job, rather than trusting to a series of names from the telephone directory.

Even people with whom they work may be glad of a recommendation, since it's hard for them to gain information which will enable them to tell a good wedding-video producer from a mediocre one. So if your customers tell you how pleased they are with the programme, have some business cards made up and ask them to pass them on to any of their friends and colleagues who are planning a wedding in the near future. You can also ask them if you can keep a copy of their programme, as you feel that something which they're so happy with could act as a good example to show other prospective customers.

But this word-of-mouth recommendation, while extremely useful for future business, will almost certainly not be enough on its own. You might feel it is worthwhile to take out an advertisement in your local business directory, or the *Yellow Pages* — and, as there won't be anything to tell you apart from your competitors, it might be worth mentioning that you have sample programmes you can show prospective customers. Few sales aids can be more convincing than a programme you have been paid to make by someone else with similar worries and similar expectations.

That's a useful starting point, but there are other ways to reach your potential customers. Keep an eye on your local paper for information on bridal fairs — where providers of every kind of wedding service, from cars to cakes, come together to market their services to couples and families with a wedding to plan. In time you may well feel it worth taking space in your own right, with a VCR and a large-screen television on which to show potential customers samples of your programmes. At the beginning of your business though, a useful step would be to make contact with service providers in different areas — a garage which runs a wedding-car service, or a stills photographer who specialises in weddings — to show them your programmes, and ask them to pass your name on to their customers.

Other useful outlets for advertising include bridal features in local newspapers, and (once you are better established) the occasional advertisement in one or more of the magazines and catalogues aimed at the wedding market. You could also try specialist bridal-wear shops and hire firms. If you can persuade them to view your sample programme, and convince them of the care and quality of your service, they should be glad to have an additional recommendation to pass onto any clients who ask them for advice in this area.

It should be clear from many of these marketing possibilities that, in all areas where your existing clients can't be there to speak on your behalf, a sample programme is the next best thing. As your experience grows along with the number of successful programmes you've made, you can be more ambitious in producing your own sales and publicity aids. For example, a single wedding video, however well you made it and however carefully you carried out that couple's wishes, still represents what one particular couple wanted. Other people may want different styles, approaches, and special effects. The other possible shortcoming of a single programme is that few potential customers are going to want to watch it all the way through. What you really need is a fast-moving selection of excerpts from as many different programmes as possible — what professional video producers call a 'showreel'.

If you decide to make yourself a showreel, treat it as just another editing assignment with yourself as the client. Keep it as short as possible — ten minutes is a good target, but five minutes of really good, varied material might be even better — and make sure your programme has a shape, to prevent viewers becoming confused with too many changes of pace and subject. A useful approach is to edit very short sequences together, choosing your best and most varied shots from your favourite wedding videos, in the order in which they would occur in a single programme. Start with bride-and-groom preparation sequences, then show a selection of church-and-ceremony excerpts, a section on the photograph session and end with assorted glimpses of receptions, together with some different special-effects sequences — and no one will be in doubt over what you can do.

A living or a hobby?

The final decision is, perhaps, the hardest of all, particularly if you come to enjoy making wedding videos. Does it offer a reasonable living to those who find they have a genuine gift for it? In many cases the answer is probably no — the market limitations mean that, unless you become very well known and can begin to raise your charges accordingly, you won't earn enough through weekend working to make the whole exercise worthwhile.

Given these circumstances, it would be far better to treat it as a useful and enjoyable source of additional income. If you can combine it with other ways of earning a living with video equipment, the idea becomes more viable again; if not, then making wedding videos could still provide cash for you to add new items of equipment to your home video studio, and to upgrade your technical capabilities as your objectives and your programmes become more ambitious. In this way, an enjoyable hobby can be made to pay for itself, while at the same time helping you improve your programmes, and the professional standards you can offer to an ever increasing circle of delighted customers.

Index